USBORNE

INTERNET-LINK

D0764500

MYSTERIES & MARVELS
OF
SCIENCE

DATE DUE

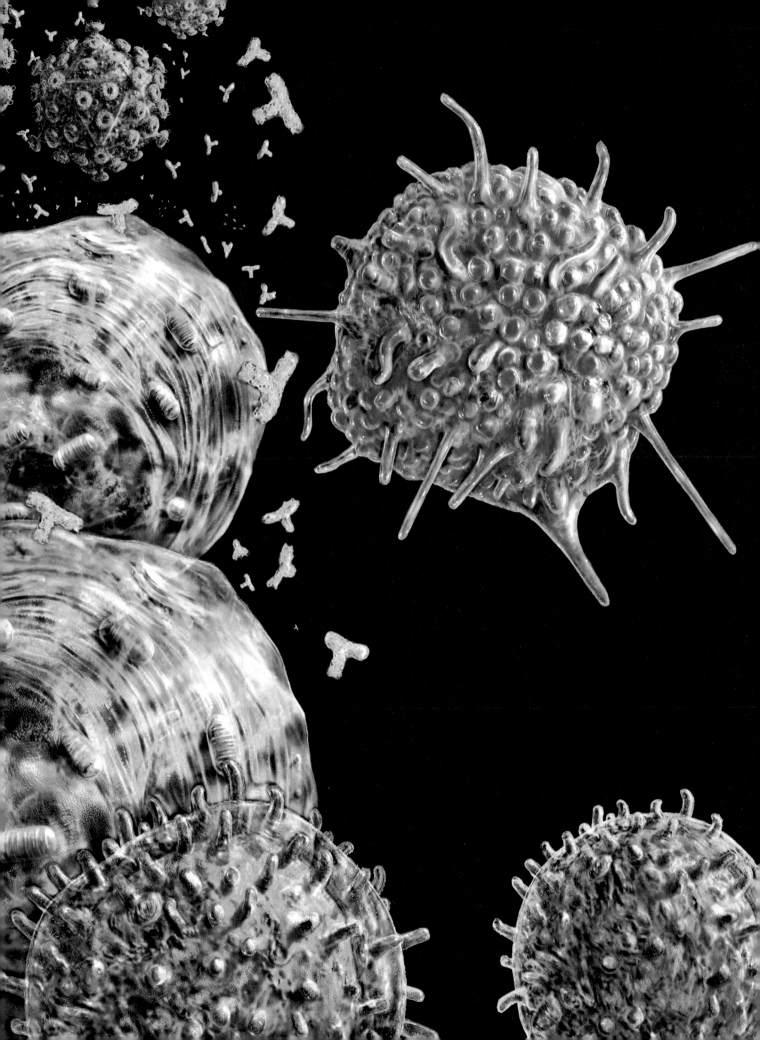

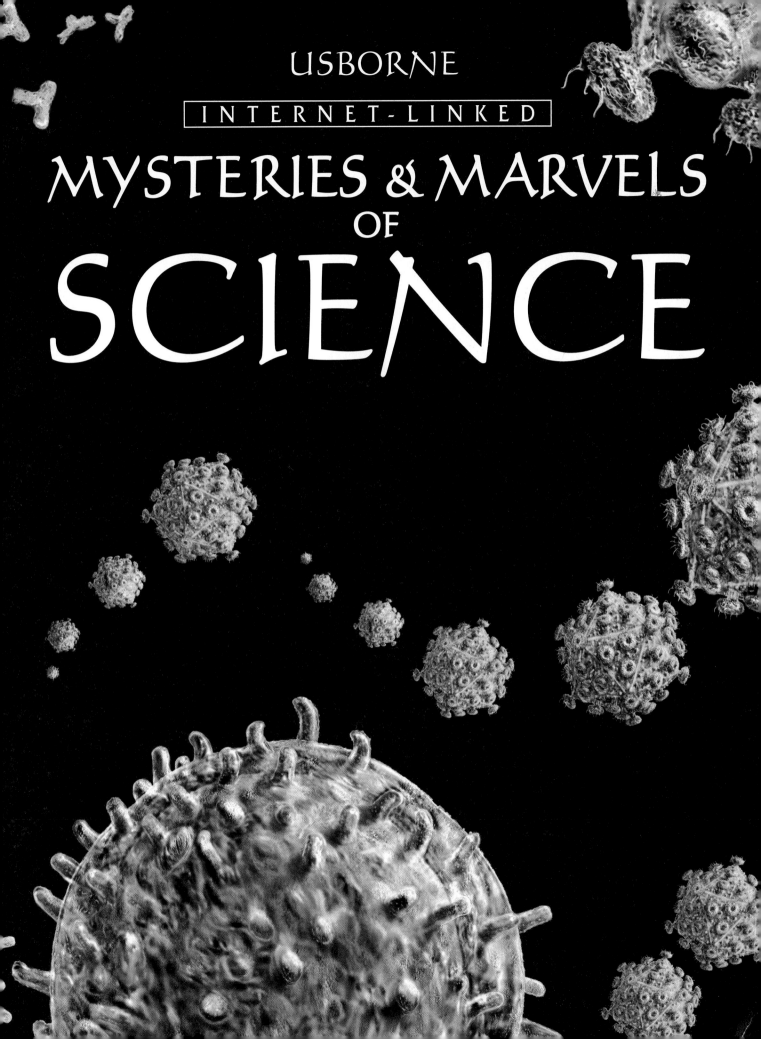

USBORNE
INTERNET-LINKED

MYSTERIES & MARVELS
OF
SCIENCE

The websites recommended in this book can be accessed via the Usborne Quicklinks
website at *www.usborne-quicklinks.com*. Usborne Publishing has made every effort to ensure
that material on the recommended sites is suitable for its intended purpose, and the sites
are regularly reviewed by Usborne editors. However, the content of a website may change
at any time, and Usborne Publishing is not responsible for the accuracy or suitability of the
information on any website other than its own. We recommend that children are
supervised while on the Internet, that they do not use Internet chat rooms, and that you
use Internet filtering software to block unsuitable material.

ISBN 0-439-78720-3

12 11 10 9 8 7 6 5 4 3 2 1   5 6 7 8 9 10/0

Printed in the U.S.A.   40

First Scholastic printing, October 2005

USBORNE
INTERNET-LINKED
MYSTERIES & MARVELS
OF
SCIENCE

Phillip Clarke, Laura Howell
and Sarah Khan

Designed by Adam Constantine, Michael Hill
and Laura Hammonds

Illustrations by Keith Furnival

Edited by Kirsteen Rogers

Consultants:
Dr Keith Taber, Revd Professor Michael J. Reiss,
Dr Tom Petersen, Dr John Rostron,
Elaine Wilson

Americanization by
Carrie Armstrong

SCHOLASTIC INC.
New York Toronto London Auckland Sydney
Mexico City New Delhi Hong Kong Buenos Aires

Internet links

Throughout this book, we have suggested interesting websites where you can find out more about science. To visit the sites, go to the Usborne Quicklinks Website at **www.usborne-quicklinks.com** and type the keywords "marvels of science". There you will find links to click on to take you to all the sites. Here are some of the things you can do on the websites:

- Build your own virtual robot and send it off on dangerous missions

- See brain-bending, animated optical illusions – and discover how they work

- Play a game that demonstrates the mysterious effects of light-speed travel

Internet safety

When using the Internet, please follow these guidelines:

- Ask your parent's or guardian's permission before you connect to the Internet.

- If you write a message in a website guest book or on a website message board, do not include any personal information such as your full name, address or telephone number, and ask an adult before you give your email address.

- If a website asks you to log in or register by typing your name or email address, ask permission of an adult first.

- If you receive an email from someone you don't know, tell an adult and do not reply to the email.

- Never arrange to meet anyone you have talked to on the Internet.

Computer not essential

If you don't have access to the Internet, don't worry. This book is a complete, self-contained reference book on its own.

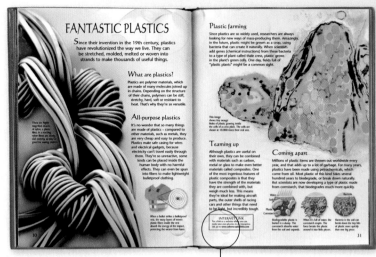

Look for descriptions of recommended websites on the pages of this book, then go to the Usborne Quicklinks Website for links to all the sites.

INTERNET LINK
For a link to a website where you can make your own plastics in an interactive lab, go to **www.usborne-quicklinks.com**

Site availability

The links in Usborne Quicklinks are regularly reviewed and updated, but occasionally you may get a message that a site is unavailable. This might be temporary, so try again later, or even the next day. If any of the sites close down, we will, if possible, replace them with suitable alternatives, so you will always find an up-to-date list of sites in Usborne Quicklinks.

Note for parents and guardians

The websites described in this book are regularly reviewed and the links in Usborne Quicklinks are updated. However, the content of a website may change at any time and Usborne Publishing is not responsible for the content on any website other than its own.

We recommend that children are supervised while on the Internet, that they do not use Internet chat rooms, and that you use Internet filtering software to block unsuitable material. Please ensure that your children read and follow the safety guidelines printed on the left. For more information, see the "Net Help" area on the Usborne Quicklinks Website.

CONTENTS

MYSTERIOUS WORLD

Why does the Sun rise? What is fire? Where do colors come from? If you're curious about the mysteries of the world, you may have the makings of a scientist. Science begins with wonder, but goes further, using reason and imagination to look for explanations.

Scientific method

Scientists investigate all sorts of things, but they all seek knowledge in the same basic way, known as scientific method. This is a well-organized version of everyday reasoning. It involves looking at the world, guessing how part of it works, predicting what should happen if your guess is right, then testing your predictions.

You notice apples falling from a tree, and wonder if heavy things hit the ground more quickly than light things. You guess they do.

You predict that a large block of modeling clay will hit the ground before a small one.

You test your idea by dropping both blocks from the same height. They hit the ground together. You were wrong, so you rethink your idea, and start a new test.

Scientists look carefully at the world, not taking for granted what they will find. This scientist is studying a frog very closely.

The homes of many sea plants and animals around the world are being destroyed by pollution. This scientist is testing a man-made structure that has become a new home for sea creatures.

All kinds

If you think that all scientists wear white coats and lurk in laboratories, then you're wrong. Scientists can be found climbing trees in the rainforest, or diving in coral reefs, discovering new animals and plants. Some are building intelligent robots, or are deep underground probing the basic particles of matter. Still others are looking back to the dawn of time, studying the birth of the universe with powerful telescopes.

Just a century ago, some scientists thought that science had few questions left to answer. Today, scientists know that they have barely begun their quest for knowledge: the world is more mysterious and marvelous than ever.

INTERNET LINKS
Have a try at being a scientist: to find links to some experiments you can try for yourself, go to www.usborne-quicklinks.com

Just a theory?

People sometimes say, "Oh, that's only a theory...," meaning that it's just a guess with no proof. To scientists, a theory is just the opposite: it's a guess that has stood the test of time. For instance, in 1686, the scientist Isaac Newton published his theory of gravity, explaining how things fall and how the planets orbit the Sun.

Newton's theory was a success for hundreds of years. Yet in the 20th century, the scientist Albert Einstein published a theory that better explains how gravity works in extreme conditions. This does not overturn Newton's theory, but it shows why even the best theories are never called facts: new evidence may always be found.

THE SMALLEST SCALE

A grain of sand seems tiny, but if you could zoom inside one, you would see that it is made up of trillions of pieces, called atoms. In fact, there are probably more atoms in a grain of sand than there are grains of sand on all the beaches of the world.

Inside atoms

All things are made of atoms, yet atoms are made up of even smaller pieces called protons, neutrons and electrons. Protons have a positive electric charge; electrons have a negative charge. Neutrons have no charge so are said to be neutral.

There are various types of atoms, and each type has a certain number of protons and electrons. In any one atom, the number of protons and electrons is equal. So, for each positive charge, there is a negative charge to cancel it out, leaving atoms with no overall charge. Sometimes atoms gain or lose electrons, and become charged particles called ions.

In the middle of an atom, particles called protons and neutrons are joined into a tight mass, called the nucleus, while electrons buzz around it.

Atoms in diagrams are often shown as solid balls. This diagram gives an idea of what's going on inside.

Atoms are mostly empty space, and this diagram isn't to scale. If an atom were the size of the Earth, its nucleus would be the size of a basketball, with cherry-sized electrons orbiting in the outer regions of the atmosphere.

Smaller still

Protons and neutrons are made up of even tinier particles called quarks, stuck tightly together by particles called gluons. There are six types (called flavors) of quark, known as up, down, top, bottom, strange and charm. Protons and neutrons are made of up and down quarks.

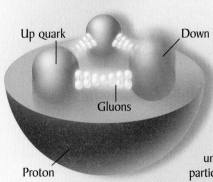

Up quark

Down quark

Gluons

Proton

Protons are made up of three smaller particles called quarks. The force that binds them together is the strongest in the universe. It is carried by particles called gluons.

This computer image shows iron atoms that have been nudged into a circle on a copper surface with a microscopic metal tip. The ripples show how electric charge is spread out across the copper.

Seeing atoms

Atoms are invisibly small, but they can be sensed, pictured, and even moved around, using a powerful tool called a scanning tunneling microscope (STM). An STM has a metal tip just a few atoms wide that scans the surface of a conductor (a material electrons can move through). The tip is given a positive electrical charge and electrons on the surface are drawn to it, creating an electric current. The strength of the current increases near the material's surface, so, by measuring the current, the STM can build up a picture of the atomic landscape.

INTERNET LINK
For a link to a website where you can build a virtual carbon atom, go to
www.usborne-quicklinks.com

An STM measures changes in electric current flowing to its tip, and so senses dips and bumps in the surface it scans.

If the tip is negatively charged, electrons on atoms below are repelled by it, allowing the atoms to be pushed around.

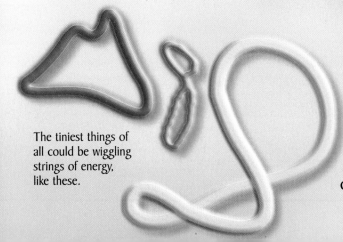

The tiniest things of all could be wiggling strings of energy, like these.

How short is a piece of string?

Some scientists think that the tiniest particles, such as quarks and electrons, are not actually little points, but are vibrations made by strings of energy, called superstrings, ten trillion times smaller. It can be helpful to think of quarks and electrons as being like different musical notes played on identical strings.

9

BUILDING BLOCKS

Substances with just one type of atom in them are called elements. There are 90 elements found in nature, like a set of building blocks from which everything is made. Each element's atoms have a unique number of protons and electrons, affecting the way it acts.

Weighty matters

Gold is one of the heaviest elements because its atoms hold so many protons and neutrons. The simplest and lightest element is hydrogen, because its atoms each have just one proton and one electron (and electrons weigh next to nothing).

Add another proton, neutron and electron to a gold atom and you have a mercury atom. All elements heavier than this have radioactive forms. Radioactive elements slowly lose particles from their atoms, breaking down into lighter, stable elements whose atoms won't break down further. For instance, the radioactive element uranium will, over billions of years, turn into a stable piece of lead.

Gold is one of the few elements that is found in nature in its pure form. Here, it is embedded in quartz crystal, which is made up of the elements silicon and oxygen.

INTERNET LINK
To find out more about the periodic table and play an elements game, go to www.usborne-quicklinks.com

Sticking together

Atoms are rarely found alone, and most elements are made up of clumps of atoms called molecules, or large networks of atoms called lattices. Atoms of one element can bond together with atoms of another to make a vast range of new substances, called compounds. The making or breaking-up of compounds is called a chemical reaction.

Helium is one of the few elements that exist as single atoms.

Oxygen atoms stick together in molecule pairs.

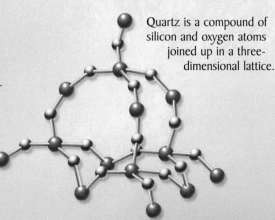

Quartz is a compound of silicon and oxygen atoms joined up in a three-dimensional lattice.

Electric connections

Many chemical reactions show signs that you can see, such as the explosion below. What you don't see is that, as the atoms rearrange and bond to form new substances, only the electrons moving across their surfaces are involved.

Electrons whizz around an atom's nucleus in a wave-like blur, but scientists find it useful to picture them grouped in shells. As atoms move closer together, electrons in one atom's outer shell are attracted to the nucleus of another. This leads to atoms bonding by giving, receiving or sharing electrons. The number of electrons in an atom's outer shell controls which atoms it will bond with. Some arrangements of electrons in shells are stable, and compounds form.

Two hydrogen atoms share electrons to form a hydrogen molecule.

Hydrogen and oxygen are explosive gases, but react to form a stable compound: water. In a water molecule, an oxygen atom gains a stable shell of eight electrons by sharing electrons with two hydrogen atoms.

Just one drop of water will start a fiery chemical reaction with a lump of potassium metal. Metal elements tend to lose electrons in reactions. Potassium atoms have just one electron to lose, so potassium reacts very easily.

Table of dreams

In 1869, a Russian chemist, Dmitri Mendeleyev, was puzzling over the 62 elements known at that time. He was trying to sort them into a table whose rows and columns of elements had things in common. One night, in a dream, he saw the answer: the table needed gaps for elements yet to be discovered. He wrote out his periodic table, as he called it, and has been proved right every time a new element has been found.

The white squares in the periodic table below show the elements discovered since Mendeleyev's day.

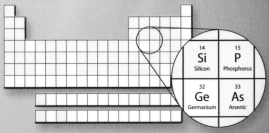

14	15
Si	P
Silicon	Phosphorus
32	33
Ge	As
Germanium	Arsenic

SMASHING ATOMS

If particles are given enough energy, they can whizz around at almost the speed of light. If they collide, the force can be so great that atoms smash apart, flinging out other particles as they do so. These sometimes join to form atoms of a new element.

Copying cosmic rays

Particle collisions happen in nature when cosmic rays, which are particles hurtling at high speeds through the Milky Way, crash into the Earth's atmosphere. Scientists who want to study particle collisions recreate them closer to home, using machines called particle accelerators. These machines use magnets and electricity to speed up particles into a frenzy until they crash into stationary targets or each other.

Spirals like these show the paths of particles through a heated liquid in a particle detector. The liquid bubbles up where the particles pass through. A computer joins up the bubbles to show them as swirly white lines.

This tube creates rapidly changing electrical fields inside a particle accelerator. These changes give the particles a repetitive series of electrical "kicks" to speed them up.

Crash detectives

Most particles that fly out after a particle collision travel only short distances before they start to break up. Keeping track of them is no easy task, so detecting equipment surrounds the crash sites in particle accelerators, recording the effects of each collision. The detectors produce pictures of the paths the particles have taken, helping scientists to work out the size, speed, charge and spin of these new particles.

INTERNET LINK
For a link to a website where you can watch animations and play games about the world's largest particle accelerator, go to **www.usborne-quicklinks.com**

Making superheavies

Scientists have created the heaviest elements ever by firing a beam of calcium atoms at a target made from americium, a metal that is most commonly used in smoke detectors. The collision created four atoms of an element that was named ununpentium.

The nucleus at the heart of each atom was crammed with 115 protons. These jostled around for space so violently that each nucleus shattered within one second, spraying out atoms of another new element. This element – which had 113 protons – was named ununtrium. Previously, the heaviest element had been Darmstadtium, with 110 protons.

This computer image shows how the world's heaviest element was created. The image shows the nucleus of a calcium atom (shown as pink) zooming towards the nucleus of an atom of americium (shown as yellow) in a particle accelerator.

Radiation zapper

Particle accelerators could be used to transform dangerous waste from nuclear power stations into harmless elements. Nuclear waste is made of unstable radioactive materials, whose atoms have so many particles moving around inside them that they give out particles. This is called high-energy radiation and can cause diseases such as cancer.

In the future, unstable radioactive materials could be zapped with beams of protons to make them split into stable elements, whose atoms contain fewer particles. These particles aren't given out but, instead, are held together inside the newly formed atoms.

Atoms of radioactive elements contain so many particles that some escape as high-energy radiation.

Bombarding radioactive atoms with proton beams changes them into atoms with fewer particles. These don't give out radiation.

CHEMICAL DETECTIVES

How can you tell one chemical from another? The way a chemical looks or smells may give you a clue to what it is. But when scientists need to identify the elements in a substance, they use their knowledge of how chemicals behave in a whole range of situations, such as when they are boiled, X-rayed or mixed with other chemicals.

Element barcodes

An element in gas form can give out colored light rays. This happens when it is heated until it glows, and the light it produces is directed through a slit and then through a glass prism. Whereas light from the Sun can be separated into all the colors of the rainbow, the light from heated elements will only separate into rays of certain colors. Each element always produces the same set of colored lines, like its own unique barcode.

Screen

Prism

Bar with slit

Heated hydrogen gas

The light from heated hydrogen gas is passed through a slit and a prism, to separate it out into rays of color.

The X factor

Scientists can identify the structure of an element by X-raying it. When X-rays pass through an element, they hit the atoms inside it. As a result of these collisions, the X-rays change direction, and come out of the element at different angles from which they entered. The change in direction tells the scientists how the atoms inside the element are arranged. With this information, they can determine what the element is.

To produce this image, X-rays were passed through a tiny piece of gold and then recorded on electronic equipment linked to a computer. The computer turned the information into this image.

Ink investigation

In 1983, German scientists analyzed the ink used in diaries claimed to have been written by the German Nazi leader Adolf Hitler. The tests were carried out to find out if the diaries were genuine.

Every type of black ink contains a unique mixture of dyes. Scientists scraped some ink off one of the pages, placed it onto blotting paper and dipped the end of the paper in alcohol. As the alcohol soaked upwards, it carried the ink with it. The particles in each dye traveled at different speeds up the paper, resulting in a sort of rainbow effect. This process revealed four different makes of ink in the diaries, none of which had been available when Hitler was alive: the diaries were proven to be fakes.

On each of these circular pieces of paper, a spot of ink has been separated out by a drop of alcohol, revealing the different dyes contained in the ink.

INTERNET LINK
For a link to a website where you can investigate ink online, go to
www.usborne-quicklinks.com

In the blood

Forensic scientists can detect poisons, alcohol and drugs in a sample of blood using a process called gas chromatography. The sample is heated and pushed through a coiled glass tube by a flow of helium or nitrogen gas. Each substance in the sample travels at a different speed, and any chemical that may have been dissolved in the blood is separated out. Computerized detectors at the end of the tube identify the separate substances.

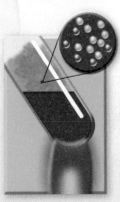

Nitrogen gas

Blood contains a mixture of substances. A sample is heated until it turns into a gas, which is collected in a syringe.

The gas is injected into a glass tube. Nitrogen gas is also pumped into the tube, where it mixes with the blood.

The nitrogen gas flows through the tube, pushing the blood along and separating out its different substances.

DESIGNER MOLECULES

Until recently, it was impossible even to see atoms and molecules, but now, scientists can move them around and put them together to build things. Rearranging molecules is the key to all kinds of new medicines, materials and technology.

DNA is a chemical that can hold lots of information, so artificial molecules of it, like this one, are perfect for making tiny computers.

Body building

Despite advances in science, nature is still the master builder on an atomic scale. Scientists make many synthetic molecules by adapting ones that already exist in the natural world. For instance, DNA is a molecule found in all living things, that contains the information to create their unique features. It normally looks like a twisted ladder, but scientists have "folded" synthetic DNA into a rigid, eight-sided ball smaller than a germ. This new shape makes it much easier to build with.

Trial and error

Creating new drugs is a very important part of molecular research. Sometimes, scientists can do this by using an existing molecule's structure as a guide to making a new one. Usually, though, it's a long process of modeling many thousands of new molecules then finding out what each one does. This method is very expensive and time-consuming, but advances in computer technology have begun to make it easier.

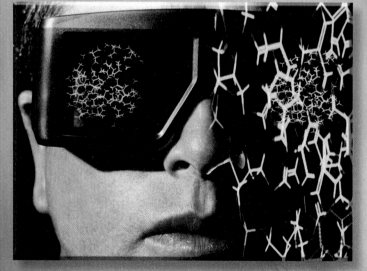

A researcher uses goggles to view computer-generated virtual molecules, which he can also move around to see what they do.

Magic bullets

Researchers are trying to build molecules into "magic bullets" – drugs that target only the affected areas of the body. They hope that one day, this will allow them to treat cancer without the severe side effects caused by many cancer fighting drugs. The answer may lie in prodrugs, molecules designed to exist harmlessly in the body until they reach a tumor.

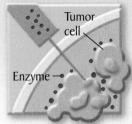
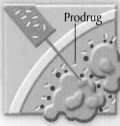

Before patients are given a prodrug, they are injected with a type of chemical called an enzyme, which attaches itself to the tumor cells.

The prodrug is like a molecular bomb which contains cell-destroying poisons. It can't go off until it makes contact with the enzyme.

The prodrug releases its poisonous contents directly into the tumor cells, which it then starts to kill. It does no harm to the rest of the body.

INTERNET LINK
For a link to a website where you can find out more about the many stages of creating a new drug, go to www.usborne-quicklinks.com

Tiny builders

In the future, molecules will be put together to make amazingly small objects, from household items to computers the size of a sugarlump. The question is, how can items that have to be built so precisely ever be mass-produced? Experts think the answer lies in microscopic robots called nanoassemblers. These incredibly small machines will use atoms not only to assemble objects, but also to make new copies of themselves. Production lines of billions of nanoassemblers could even be sent to other planets to construct space stations on their surface.

This computer image shows a miniature robot assembler grabbing bacteria in its claws. It will use these as raw materials to build more robots like itself.

17

MATTER ON THE MOVE

Everything around us is made of matter, but why are some things solid as a rock, while others flow like maple syrup or vanish like a puff of steam?

Sluggish solids

Most of the matter you see around you is solid: the house you live in, the chairs you sit on, the books you read – even the tiny specks of dust floating in the air. But what makes matter solid?

All matter is made up of tiny, moving particles called atoms, or clumps of atoms called molecules, which are drawn to each other by electrical forces. Molecules in solids don't have much energy, so, while they may joggle slightly, they stay in the same spot – similar to someone running in place. This means that solid matter stays in the same shape.

This splashing water drop shows that, although liquids have no fixed shape, they take on many shapes as they move.

INTERNET LINK
For a link to a website where you can find out more about atoms, molecules and the states of matter, go to www.usborne-quicklinks.com

Go with the flow

When a solid is heated to a certain level, its molecules gain enough energy to move around more freely. The solid matter then melts into a liquid: its molecules flow easily around each other, and it loses its fixed shape. A liquid's molecules are still drawn to each other, though, so they stay together, the liquid filling a fixed amount of space. Liquids take the shape of any container they are in.

The molecules in solid objects have little energy, so they stay in the same place.

Inside a body of liquid, the molecules have enough energy to move around each other.

It's a gas

When liquids are heated enough, their molecules gain the energy to overcome the electrical forces that keep them together. The liquid then boils: its molecules fly free from its surface and it becomes a gas. Gases spread out to fill any space they are in. Unless they are kept in a tightly sealed container they will escape.

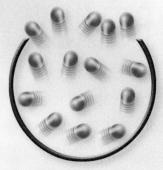

The energetic molecules in gases move freely, and spread out to fill any space they are in.

Breaking free

The positively charged nucleus in the middle of an atom has negatively charged electrons whizzing around it. The electrical force that attracts opposite charges stops the electrons from flying off, and also joins atoms into molecules. If a gas becomes extremely hot, the atoms in its molecules gain enough energy to overcome the pull of the electrical force, and split apart from each other. Then the electrons become energetic enough to break free from the atoms. A cloud of electrons, and atoms that have lost them (ions), is formed. This is called a plasma.

In plasmas, electrons escape from their atoms. As this happens, the atoms become charged, and are called ions.

The huge amounts of energy needed to turn gas into plasma are not commonly found on Earth, but plasma does form briefly in flashes of lightning. There is a little plasma in fire, and inside fluorescent tubes, but most is found out in space. Stars, such as the Sun, are huge balls of plasma, and space itself is strewn with shining plasma clouds called bright nebulas. In fact, of the four states of matter, solids, liquids and gases make up only 1% of matter in the universe: all the rest is plasma.

These glowing streamers are plasma being created inside a glass sphere. Atoms of neon gas are being heated and ripped apart by a huge build-up of electrical charge, giving off energy in the form of pink light.

CRYSTALS

Most pure solid substances, from grains of salt to the most precious gemstones, are made up of flat-faced, straight-sided shapes called crystals.

Salt crystals are cube-shaped because the tiny particles that make them up are arranged in repeating, cube-shaped patterns.

Little goes large

The shape of crystals can vary from one substance to another. This is because the particles inside them are built up in different ways. The atoms, ions or molecules in crystals are ordered in repeating patterns called lattices, which are echoed from this tiny scale all the way up to the full-size crystal.

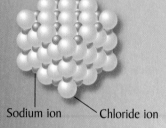

Sodium ion   Chloride ion

A typical grain of salt contains 100,000 trillion ions arranged in a cubic lattice, like the one shown here.

Crystal crowns

Crystals appear in all sorts of natural substances, even in living things, such as microscopic viruses. Viruses are simple life-forms that live inside the cells of animals and plants. Their heads are made of a single crystal, often a 20-sided shape called an icosahedron.

These three viruses are on the surface of a much larger cell, which will help them to reproduce. The crystal shape of their heads is clear to see.

INTERNET LINK
For a link to a website where you can play some liquid crystal games, go to **www.usborne-quicklinks.com**

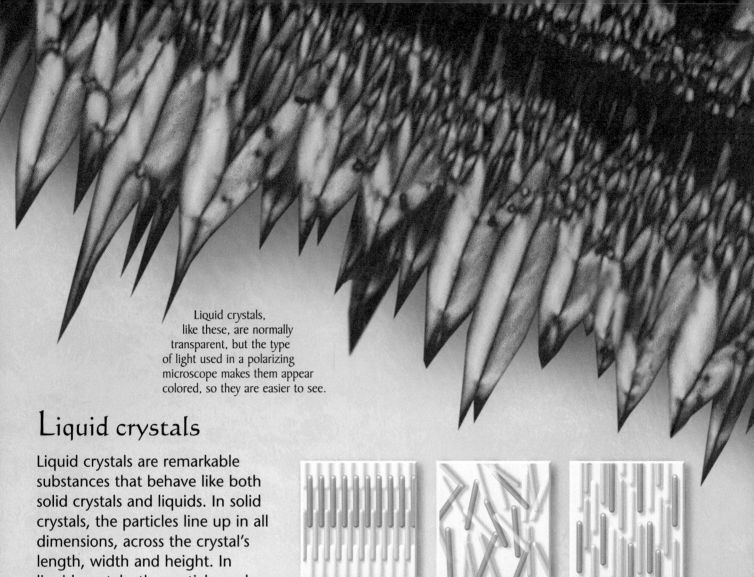

Liquid crystals, like these, are normally transparent, but the type of light used in a polarizing microscope makes them appear colored, so they are easier to see.

Liquid crystals

Liquid crystals are remarkable substances that behave like both solid crystals and liquids. In solid crystals, the particles line up in all dimensions, across the crystal's length, width and height. In liquid crystals, the particles only line up in one dimension: in other dimensions the particles can move freely, as they would in a liquid.

In a solid crystal, the molecules are lined up and locked rigidly in a fixed position.

In a liquid, the position of molecules isn't fixed, so they are able to move around freely.

In a liquid crystal, the molecules are able to move around, but only in a single direction.

When light shines through liquid crystals, it follows the direction of their molecules. If an electric current is passed through the crystals, the molecules twist around, blocking the light. This effect is used to create images on liquid crystal displays (LCDs), as on digital watches or flat computer screens.

Crystals in space

The way crystals form is affected by the force of gravity pressing down on them. In low gravity, crystals grow bigger, better and more quickly than on Earth. Scientists are using the low gravity conditions in the Space Shuttle to grow crystals of proteins – complex molecules central to the growth of living things. Studying space-grown crystals of the protein insulin, for example, may help to develop better treatments for the condition diabetes.

These insulin crystals were grown on Earth.

These bigger ones were grown in space.

21

MIXING IT UP

From the air you breathe to many of the foods you eat, nearly all the substances around you are mixtures of elements and compounds jumbled together without being chemically linked.

Millions of mixtures

The number of possible mixtures of elements and compounds is uncountable. Some mixtures have parts that can be seen by the naked eye, for example, a jar of assorted hard candies. Others, like wet sand, have tinier ingredients: sand grains and microscopic water molecules. Many other mixtures contain just atoms and molecules. The air around you, for example, is an invisible mixture of gases.

As mixtures are not chemically bound, they can be separated fairly easily. Hard candies are easily sorted. Wet sand can be dried out and its water collected. Even air can be separated by cooling it in a laboratory and collecting its gases as they turn to liquid at very low, but different, temperatures.

Air is a mixture of gases; mainly the elements nitrogen, oxygen and argon. (In reality, the particles would be much more spaced out than shown here.)

🔵 Nitrogen 🔵 Oxygen 🔵 Argon

Vanishing act

When sugar is stirred into water, it seems to melt away and vanish. But sugar doesn't melt until it is much hotter than boiling water, so where does it go? The sugar has not melted, but dissolved: its individual molecules have spread throughout the water to make a mixture called a sugar solution. Solutions are the most finely blended of mixtures, and are always see-through, although some, such as mouthwash, have a colored tint.

As this sugar lump dissolves, the sugar disappears into a syrupy flow that slowly spreads through the water.

Polystyrene foam is 95% air, mixed with just 5% polystyrene. This microscope image shows clumps of air-filled polystyrene bubbles (yellow) separated by air-filled gaps (black).

Kept in suspense

Some substances won't mix as thoroughly as sugar and water; others hardly mix at all. In salad dressing, for instance, oil floats on vinegar. When you shake salad dressing before using it, tiny blobs of oil are suspended in the vinegar, turning it into a cloudy liquid called an emulsion. Milk and mayonnaise are other examples of emulsions.

Mixtures may also contain substances in different states. Bread and polystyrene are solids containing trapped gas bubbles. Smoke is a gas carrying soot particles.

Milk contains droplets of fat hanging in water.

Bread is a solid containing bubbles of air.

Smoke is made up of pieces of soot floating in gas.

INTERNET LINK
To find a website that tells you how to make some weird slime mixtures that are both solid and liquid, go to www.usborne-quicklinks.com

Liquid lenses

Scientists have used two liquids that don't easily mix to invent a camera lens that changes shape, like the lens in the human eye. The lens is made up of an oil and a solution in a little plastic cylinder.

When the sides of the cylinder are charged with an electric current, the solution shrinks into a dome shape at one end. The surface where the oil and the solution meet acts as a lens. As the current changes, the lens changes shape, letting it focus at different distances.

This little camera lens uses non-mixing liquids to mimic the lens in the human eye.

STRANGE MATTER

INTERNET LINKS
For links to websites about dark matter and antimatter, go to
www.usborne-quicklinks.com

Nature is never as simple as you might like. Scientists are starting to discover that everyday matter, made of atoms, ions and molecules, is just a small part of the stuff that makes up the universe.

Scientists make antimatter by blasting atoms with gamma rays. This image shows the spiraling path (green) of an electron in a particle detector, as it spins off in the opposite direction to its positron antiparticle (red). The long, green track belongs to another electron.

Mirror matter

You may have heard of strange stuff called antimatter in science fiction movies – but it is science fact. Every type of matter particle has a mirror image, or antiparticle. For instance, the electron's antiparticle is the positron. It has the same mass but opposite features, such as charge.

If a particle hits its antiparticle, they are both destroyed in a burst of energy. Particles and antiparticles are created and destroyed all the time in cosmic rays, which bombard Earth from space. Scientists can make microscopic amounts of antimatter in the laboratory. They hope to make enough to power spacecraft: just a teaspoonful could send a rocket to Mars.

Mind maps

Antimatter can be used to watch people think. In PET (positron emission tomography) brain scans, radioactive sugar called FDG is injected into the brain. The brain uses energy from sugar to work, so the parts that are thinking use up the most sugar. The FDG releases antimatter positrons from these active parts of the brain. These meet their electron opposites in the brain and are destroyed, turning into waves of energy called gamma rays. These rays are detected to build up a computer map of the brain.

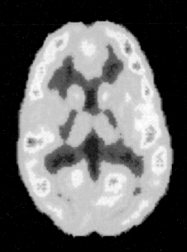

PET scans use antimatter to create a computer map of the brain. The red and yellow patches on this scan show parts the brain involved in listening to music

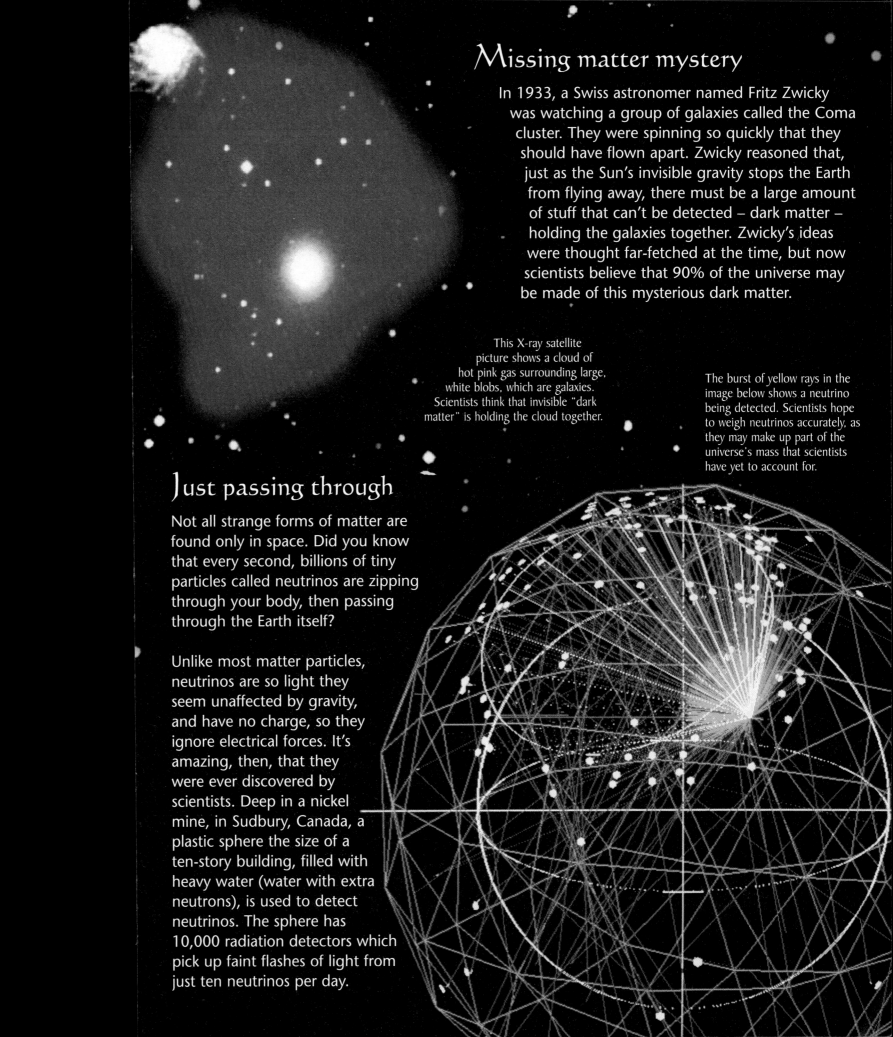

Missing matter mystery

In 1933, a Swiss astronomer named Fritz Zwicky was watching a group of galaxies called the Coma cluster. They were spinning so quickly that they should have flown apart. Zwicky reasoned that, just as the Sun's invisible gravity stops the Earth from flying away, there must be a large amount of stuff that can't be detected – dark matter – holding the galaxies together. Zwicky's ideas were thought far-fetched at the time, but now scientists believe that 90% of the universe may be made of this mysterious dark matter.

This X-ray satellite picture shows a cloud of hot pink gas surrounding large, white blobs, which are galaxies. Scientists think that invisible "dark matter" is holding the cloud together.

The burst of yellow rays in the image below shows a neutrino being detected. Scientists hope to weigh neutrinos accurately, as they may make up part of the universe's mass that scientists have yet to account for.

Just passing through

Not all strange forms of matter are found only in space. Did you know that every second, billions of tiny particles called neutrinos are zipping through your body, then passing through the Earth itself?

Unlike most matter particles, neutrinos are so light they seem unaffected by gravity, and have no charge, so they ignore electrical forces. It's amazing, then, that they were ever discovered by scientists. Deep in a nickel mine, in Sudbury, Canada, a plastic sphere the size of a ten-story building, filled with heavy water (water with extra neutrons), is used to detect neutrinos. The sphere has 10,000 radiation detectors which pick up faint flashes of light from just ten neutrinos per day.

WONDERFUL WATER

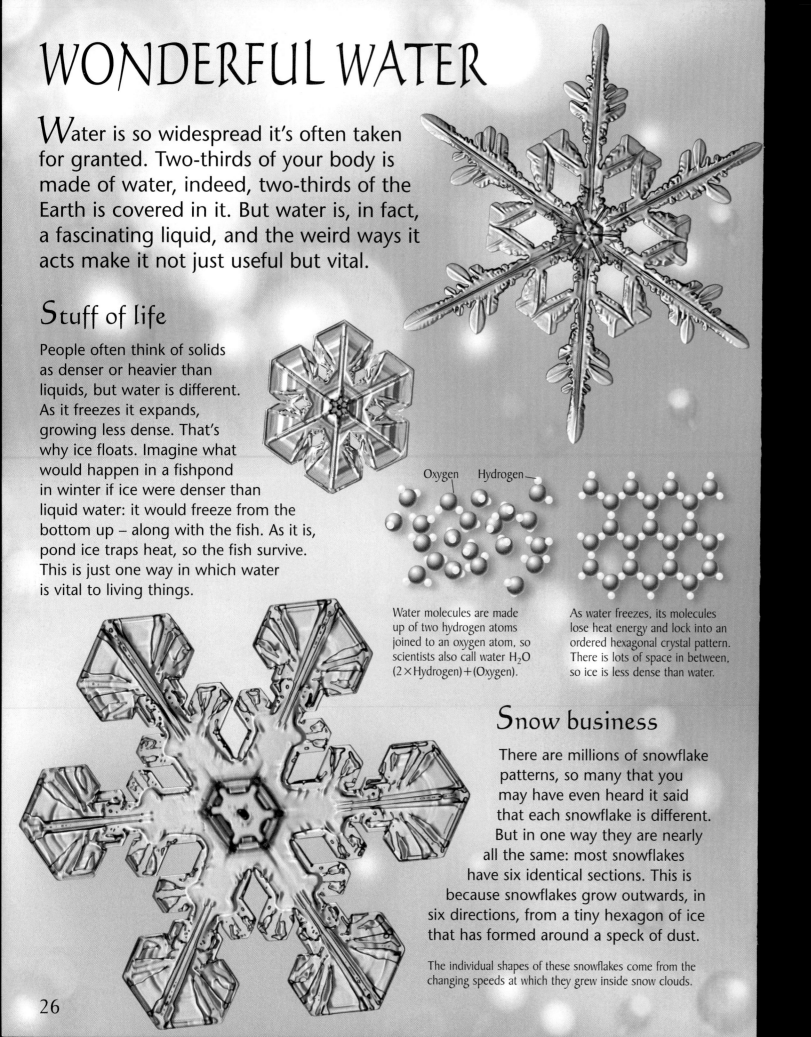

Water is so widespread it's often taken for granted. Two-thirds of your body is made of water, indeed, two-thirds of the Earth is covered in it. But water is, in fact, a fascinating liquid, and the weird ways it acts make it not just useful but vital.

Stuff of life

People often think of solids as denser or heavier than liquids, but water is different. As it freezes it expands, growing less dense. That's why ice floats. Imagine what would happen in a fishpond in winter if ice were denser than liquid water: it would freeze from the bottom up – along with the fish. As it is, pond ice traps heat, so the fish survive. This is just one way in which water is vital to living things.

Oxygen Hydrogen

Water molecules are made up of two hydrogen atoms joined to an oxygen atom, so scientists also call water H_2O ($2 \times$ Hydrogen)+(Oxygen).

As water freezes, its molecules lose heat energy and lock into an ordered hexagonal crystal pattern. There is lots of space in between, so ice is less dense than water.

Snow business

There are millions of snowflake patterns, so many that you may have even heard it said that each snowflake is different. But in one way they are nearly all the same: most snowflakes have six identical sections. This is because snowflakes grow outwards, in six directions, from a tiny hexagon of ice that has formed around a speck of dust.

The individual shapes of these snowflakes come from the changing speeds at which they grew inside snow clouds.

Liquid skin

Look at a water drop and you'll see it is shaped like a dome, as if it were held together by a transparent skin. Inside the drop, water molecules are drawn together by electrical forces like little magnets. The molecules at the surface are far more attracted to each other than to air molecules around them. This means the surface molecules hold tightly together, making the water's surface act like a stretchy skin.

This surface tension tries to pull water into the smallest shape it can: a sphere. On bodies of water larger than a drop, the force of gravity squashes the sphere flat.

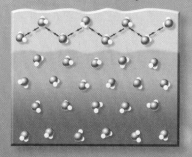

Molecules at the surface of water attract each other, making a 'skin'.

INTERNET LINK
For a link to a website where you can see amazing snowflakes, go to www.usborne-quicklinks.com

This raft spider can walk on water, held up by a liquid skin. See how the skin bends under the spider's weight.

Just add water

From powder paint to instant soup, water can dissolve more substances than any other. This is because water molecules have ends with positive and negative charges, a little like magnets. Many substances contain charged particles (ions) that are attracted to these charges. This tears the substances apart. Water's dissolving powers are vital for living things. For example, water in blood carries dissolved sugar to organs that need energy.

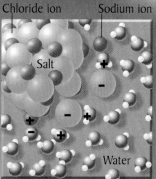

Chloride ion   Sodium ion

Salt is made up of sodium and chloride ions. The charges on water molecules tug at them, pulling the salt crystal apart.

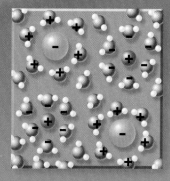

The water molecules keep pulling the sodium and chloride ions away until they are all surrounded. The salt is now dissolved in the water.

27

METAL MARVELS

Metal is one of the most useful and widely found types of materials on Earth. The chances are that, no matter where you are, there's something made of metal nearby. There's even metal in your own body.

What can metals do?

Almost all metals have features that make them useful to us: electricity can flow easily through all of them, and many can be molded, bent, beaten into sheets or stretched into wire. A few, such as iron, can be magnetized. When tiny iron particles are added to water or oil they make MR (magneto-rheological) fluid, which turns from a liquid to a solid if exposed to a magnetic field. It's very useful for strengthening buildings and bridges, as explained below.

These shiny blobs are drops of mercury, the only metal that's a liquid at room temperature.

INTERNET LINK
For a link to a website where you can take part in an animated quiz to discover some amazing uses of metals, go to www.usborne-quicklinks.com

The support cables of this bridge in China have MR fluid shock absorbers between them. Tiny iron particles float in this fluid.

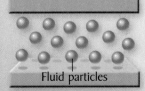

Fluid particles

If sensors in the bridge detect vibrations from wind or earthquakes, powerful magnets around the floating particles switch on and off.

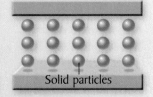

Solid particles

When the magnets are on, the fluid turns solid. It can switch instantly between the two states, allowing the cables to absorb any vibrations.

Memory metals

Scientists have found ways to give some metals even more useful features. Memory metals, for instance, return to their original shape after they have been twisted, hammered or pulled. They are useful in surgery because they can be bent and placed into awkward-to-reach parts of the body. When body heat warms the metal up, it returns to its correct shape.

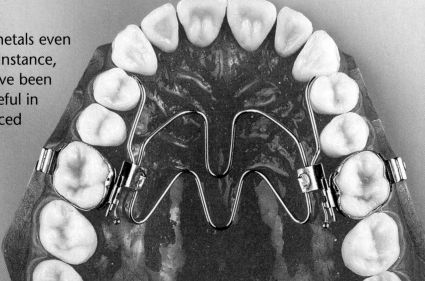

Tooth braces made of bent memory metal change shape very slowly, gently moving the teeth as they do so.

All puffed up

We think of metal as mainly being heavy and solid, but it can be melted into a liquid, then blown into foam by adding bubbles of gas. When it cools and solidifies, pockets of air are trapped inside, making it like a sponge.

Metal foam has a spongy texture like normal foam, but it's much tougher. It is heat-resistant, strong, and excellent at absorbing impacts, such as in car crashes.

Metallic meals

Metal is so important, we literally couldn't survive without it. All plants and animals have minute traces of metals in them, which they need to stay alive. For example, around 2% of a person's entire body weight is a metal called calcium, almost all of which is in the teeth and bones. Plants take in metals from soil and water, and we absorb these metals when we eat plants, or animals that ate plants.

Ores and more

Most metals can be extracted from the ground, where they exist combined with other elements, as ores. These are mined, then broken down by chemicals or exposed to electricity or fierce heat to release the metals within them. A few metals, such as gold, can exist on their own because they're so unreactive, but they're more rare than normal metals.

This ancient Egyptian mask has kept its shine for thousands of years. Gold doesn't react with air and become duller the way iron and silver do.

FANTASTIC PLASTICS

Since their invention in the 19th century, plastics have revolutionized the way we live. They can be stretched, molded, melted or woven into strands to make thousands of useful things.

What are plastics?

Plastics are polymer materials, which are made of many molecules joined up in chains. Depending on the structure of their chains, polymers can be stiff, stretchy, hard, soft or resistant to heat. That's why they're so versatile.

All-purpose plastics

It's no wonder that so many things are made of plastics – compared to other materials, such as metals, they are very cheap and easy to produce. Plastics make safe casing for wires and electrical gadgets, because electricity can't travel easily through them. They're so unreactive, some kinds can be placed inside the human body with no harmful effects. They can even be spun into fibers to make lightweight bulletproof clothing.

These are highly magnified strands of nylon, a plastic fiber, in a stocking. Nylon fibers are strong and stretchy, so they're good for making clothes.

When a bullet strikes a bulletproof vest, the many layers of woven plastic fibers inside the vest absorb the energy of the impact, protecting the wearer from harm.

Plastic farming

Since plastics are so widely used, researchers are always looking for new ways of mass-producing them. Amazingly, in the future, plastic might be grown as a crop, using bacteria that can create it naturally. When scientists add genes (chemical instructions) from these bacteria to a type of plant called thale cress, plastic grows in the plant's green cells. One day, fields full of "plastic plants" might be a common sight.

This image shows tiny orange blobs of plastic growing inside the cells of a cress plant. The cells are shown at 10,000 times their real size.

Teaming up

Although plastics are useful on their own, they can be combined with materials such as carbon, metal or glass to make even better materials called composites. One of the most ingenious features of plastic composites is that they have the strength of the materials they are combined with, but weigh much less. This means they're ideal for making aircraft parts, the outer shells of racing cars and other things that need to be light, but incredibly tough.

INTERNET LINK
For a link to a website where you can make your own plastics in an interactive lab, go to www.usborne-quicklinks.com

Coming apart

Millions of plastic items are thrown out worldwide every year, and that adds up to a lot of garbage. For many years, plastics have been made using petrochemicals, which come from oil. Most plastic of this kind takes several hundred years to biodegrade, or break down naturally. But scientists are now developing a type of plastic made from cornstarch, that biodegrades much more quickly.

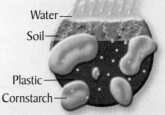

Water
Soil

Plastic
Cornstarch

Biodegradable plastic is buried in a dump. The cornstarch absorbs water from the soil and expands.

When it's full of water, the cornstarch erupts. The force breaks the plastic around it into little pieces.

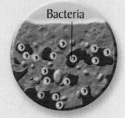

Bacteria

Bacteria in the soil can break down the tiny bits of plastic more quickly than one big piece.

31

COOL CARBON

Carbon is a real wonder element. It is found throughout the universe in suns, in planets' atmospheres, and in living things. An average person contains 16kg (35lb) of carbon combined with other elements.

Kinds of carbon

Pure carbon has three very different basic forms: graphite, diamond and fullerenes, such as Buckminsterfullerine (also called buckyballs). Soft, flaky graphite is probably best known as the "lead" in a pencil. Diamond, on the other hand, is the hardest substance in nature. A diamond-tipped drill can cut through granite as easily as a saw cuts through wood.

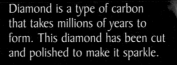

In graphite, the atoms link up like layers of chicken wire. The layers move smoothly over each other, making graphite a good lubricant. Electricity can also flow through it easily.

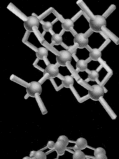

A diamond's atoms are more closely packed together than in any other substance. This is what gives diamonds their incredible hardness.

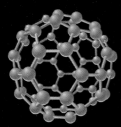

The atoms in buckyballs form a hollow ball. Their unusual structure makes them immensely strong – a hundred times stronger than steel, but only one-sixth of its weight.

Diamond is a type of carbon that takes millions of years to form. This diamond has been cut and polished to make it sparkle.

The molecule of life

Life as we know it couldn't exist without carbon. The chemicals that make up living things are incredibly complex, and only carbon can form bonds with other atoms in enough combinations to create them. So if life exists elsewhere in the universe, it is probably carbon-based too – in fact, some scientists think that the carbon that everyone is made of was created in the hearts of distant stars.

Tiny technology

Nanotechnology is the science of extremely small things. Nanomaterials, which are less than ten-thousandths of a millimeter in size, can be used to build on a tinier scale than ever before. Microscopic graphite cylinders called nanotubes are a type of nanomaterial that will be widely used in the future. They can be added to other materials to give them unbeatable strength, or used to make electronic devices 100 times smaller than today's.

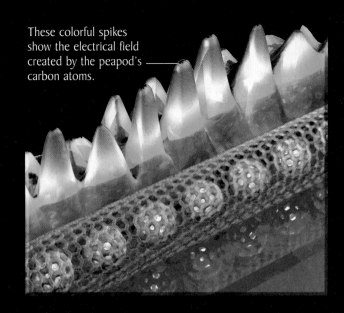

These colorful spikes show the electrical field created by the peapod's carbon atoms.

The image on the right is a computer model of a "peapod," a nanotube that's been filled with buckyballs to increase its strength.

INTERNET LINK
For a link to a website where you can see what new materials you can make from virtual carbon, go to **www.usborne-quicklinks.com**

Carbon dating

Carbon-14 is a radioactive form of carbon found in the air and in natural objects, such as wood and bones. Like all radioactive materials, it breaks down into smaller amounts over time. Every 5,700 or so years, there is half as much carbon-14 in an object as there was before. Scientists can learn how old something is by comparing the amount of carbon-14 left in it with the amount that was originally there, a technique known as carbon dating.

This is the mummified body of a man. By measuring the amount of radioactive carbon-14 it contains, scientists have worked out that he lived around 2,000 years ago.

STUNNING SILICON

Silicon is the second most common element on Earth. Combined with other elements, it makes all kinds of materials that can be used for building, storing data or traveling into space. Silicon is most commonly used in making glass.

This highly magnified image shows a microscopic creature called a diatom. Its body is protected by a hard, glassy case made of silica, with intricate patterns on its surface.

Nature's glass

We normally think of glass as an artificial material, but nature made it first. In fact, some living things, such as the water creature in the picture above, have a natural glass called silica in their bodies. Silica, a combination of silicon and oxygen, is also the main ingredient of obsidian, a glassy rock formed in the searing heat of volcanoes.

Shiny black obsidian stones like this one were originally liquid rock, which flowed out of an erupting volcano and cooled rapidly.

Man-made glass

For at least 9,000 years, people have been using sand, a mineral containing silica, to make glass. It was originally just a decorative material, but today glass has many more uses, enabling people to light their homes, transmit information and see well. The feature of glass that makes it so suitable for all these jobs is its transparency. In fact, the type of glass inside fiber-optic cables, very fine glass tubes which are used for communication, is pure and clear enough to make a window several miles thick that would still be perfectly see-through.

Chips with that?

Extremely thin slices of silicon are etched with millions of microscopic components, called transistors, to make computer microchips. As technology advances, computers need more and more transistors on each microchip to hold information. Eventually, etching won't be able to produce transistors which are small enough, so scientists have found a way to imprint more intricate chips than ever before using a laser.

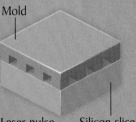

Mold | Laser pulse | Silicon slice

To make a computer chip, a silicon slice is placed next to a tiny quartz mold shaped like many transistors, with features as tiny as one hundred thousandth of the width of a human hair.

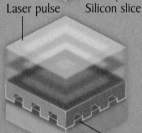

Melted silicon

A laser pulse is shone through the quartz for 20 billionths of a second, melting the top layer of silicon.

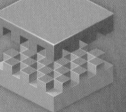

When it cools, the silicon is left imprinted with the mold's shape.

Silicate ceramics

Many years ago, people found that baking silicate minerals such as clay and feldspar turned them into hard ceramics that did not wear out with age. These were traditionally used to make bricks and tableware but today, ceramics have more hi-tech uses too, from super-sharp knives to engine parts and rocket nose cones. The Space Shuttle is protected from temperatures of up to 1,600°C (2,912°F) by a layer of ceramic tiles.

INTERNET LINK
For a link to a website where you can find fun facts and videos about glass, aerogel and silicon crystals, go to www.usborne-quicklinks.com

Hit and mist

Aerogel is an ultra-light man-made material. It contains silica, but most of it – 99.8% – is air, which makes it look like a transparent mist. Despite its ghostly appearance, it's both solid to the touch and very heat-resistant. When tiny objects hit aerogel, they become embedded in it, so NASA scientists use it to collect debris from the tails of comets to bring back to Earth and study.

Aerogel looks very delicate, but it is strong enough to support this glass dish and pile of matches, protecting them from the hot, blue flame of burning gas.

NATURE'S IDEAS

For hundreds of years, people have been trying
to create materials that meet the demands of
their basic needs and changing lifestyles. Although
many of these materials are created in a lab, the
inspiration is often provided by nature.

Nature knows best

All living creatures, including
humans, face challenges. Animals
and plants cope with difficulties
in surprisingly ingenious ways,
sometimes using natural materials
that amaze and baffle scientists.
For instance, mussels stick
themselves to rocks using a
natural, waterproof glue in their
bodies that's stronger than any
man-made glue in existence.

The shell on the right is lined with mother-of-pearl, a natural
ceramic. This contains a mix of chemicals that gives it 3,000
times more strength than the chalk that the shell is mostly
made of. Scientists still don't know how that's possible.

INTERNET LINKS
For a link to websites where you can study many
different materials and find out what it takes to be a
materials scientist, go to **www.usborne-quicklinks.com**

Finding the answer

Scientists often make discoveries by
asking, "How do other living things deal
with this problem, and how can we copy
them?" Using science to imitate nature
is called biomimicry, and it often finds
solutions in the most unlikely places.
Imagine, for example, that you wanted
to develop a material that's waterproof
and self-cleaning. Scientists have found
that lotus leaves possess both of these
properties, so they set about unlocking
the secret of how they work.

When rainwater falls on a lotus
plant leaf, the water forms a ball
and rolls off, taking dirt with it. The
leaf stays dry and clean – but how?

The answer lies in the leaf's highly
waterproof waxy coating. Scientists
learned its recipe, and are mass-
producing a synthetic version.

36

Gecko glue

Geckos are a type of lizard with the ability to cling to surfaces at any angle, even upside-down. They do this using electrically charged hairs on the soles of their feet, which are attracted to anything they touch. A material with such strong stickiness would be useful to humans, so scientists have created "gecko tape" – a strip of plastic covered in millions of synthetic hairs, like a gecko's foot – and on a smaller scale, nano-velcro.

This image shows the pads made of millions of tiny hairs which give a gecko's feet their super sticking power.

Nano-velcro, made of tiny hooked carbon tubes (nanotubes), mimics the gecko's hairs. It is 30 times more powerful than normal glue.

Super silk

Spider silk is one of nature's most marvellous materials – a lightweight fiber that's five times stronger, weight for weight, than steel. Scientists want to use these properties in synthetic materials, but the silk is hard to make in bulk. So far, they have found a way to mass-produce silk-making chemicals in the milk of some goats, by changing the goats' body chemistry.

These mushroom-shaped mounds are spinnerets, the parts of a spider's body that silk comes from. Fresh silk (shown here in blue) is oozing out.

INVESTIGATING ENERGY

What's everywhere, but can't be seen? What do you use all the time, but hardly ever notice? The answer is energy – the thing that is needed to make every action in the universe happen.

INTERNET LINK
For a link to a website where you can help a mad scientist create a monster by saving energy, go to
www.usborne-quicklinks.com

What can energy do?

Energy can do literally everything. Machines need it to function, living things need it to live, and no movement can take place without it. Different kinds of energy include light, sound and heat.

When you strike a match, it makes heat and light energy. Before the match was struck, though, that energy was stored in the chemicals on its head.

Eternal energy

If energy is everywhere, making things happen, where does it come from, and what happens if it runs out? Actually, all the energy that exists now was created at the same time as the universe itself. It never gets used up, just moved around – for instance, when coal is burned in power stations to make electrical energy. But this energy isn't new: it already existed inside the coal.

Millions of years ago, the Earth was covered with plants. They grew using energy from the Sun.

The plants died with the energy stored inside them. Over time, their remains were crushed under the ground and became coal.

Today, coal is burned to release the energy that was trapped inside the plants all those years ago.

All change

Energy can never be created or destroyed, only changed from one form to another. This is called the Law of Conservation of Energy. Whenever any action takes place, energy is being changed.

Hold a pencil in the air. Chemical energy from food in your body turns into kinetic (movement) energy as you raise your arm.

The pencil now has potential energy, because it has been lifted against the force of gravity: if you drop it, it will fall.

As it drops, the pencil has kinetic energy. When it hits the ground, this becomes sound energy, and you hear a noise.

Energy unleashed

An enormous amount of energy is stored in the heart of every atom. It's called nuclear energy, because it is released when the nucleus of an atom is split apart. Unlike other reactions, where one type of energy is converted to another, nuclear reactions make energy from matter. This is possible because matter is like stored energy, in that it too cannot be created or destroyed.

The physicist Albert Einstein determined that a very small amount of mass, another word for matter, can be made into a vast amount of energy. That's how nuclear power works – atoms of a nuclear fuel, such as uranium, are split inside a reactor to release the stores of energy inside them.

This pool-type nuclear reactor, used for research and training, produces much less energy than a power plant.

The pool water keeps the reactor core stable.

POWER TO THE PEOPLE

Over the years, people have come to depend on more and more energy to provide heat, light, electricity and transport. Most of this energy comes from burning fossil fuels such as gas, oil and coal. But these won't last forever.

INTERNET LINK
For a link to a website where you can play games about power, go to **www.usborne-quicklinks.com**

Fuels of the future

Experts think that before this century ends, there will be no oil or gas left. The race is on to find the best alternatives for a fossil fuel-free future. Renewable energy sources like the ones on this page are a good option, as they won't ever run out. But most of them are limited as to where or how they can be used. Scientists are constantly looking for cheaper, cleaner and more convenient sources of renewable energy.

This is a wind farm in California. A device called a turbine changes movement energy from these giant blades into electrical energy. Wind power is one of many alternatives to fossil fuel.

Cleaner cars

People's power needs aren't limited to electricity for homes and workplaces. Cars and other vehicles use fossil fuels too, releasing damaging gases into the atmosphere as they go. Ideally, vehicles of the future need to run on a clean, plentiful power source that doesn't hurt the environment. With this in mind, scientists have developed hydrogen fuel cells. Hydrogen gas is freely available, and creates no harmful exhaust fumes.

Hydrogen

Oxygen

Water molecules

Inside a fuel cell, hydrogen and oxygen atoms join together and release energy. The only by-product of this chemical reaction is H_2O – ordinary water.

Natural energy

Living things gain the energy that they use to grow from the Sun, which makes them miniature powerhouses – as long as you can find a way to use them. Landfills, farming and some kinds of industrial processes, such as paper-making, all produce large amounts of energy-filled natural matter. Also known as biomass, this mostly consists of dung, dead plants and wood pulp. To release its energy it can be burned as it is, or processed into chemical fuels such as ethanol.

Biomass energy can come from any natural source – including animals' bodies. In some countries, animal dung is widely used as a fuel.

Cow dung is gathered, mixed with straw and left to dry. These dung pancakes can then be burned to heat homes or make cooking fires.

Plasma power

Today's nuclear power plants produce energy by breaking down atoms, but one day they may use nuclear fusion – that is, joining atoms together. Fusion releases huge amounts of energy in the form of unimaginably hot plasma. In theory, fusion plasma could provide the whole world with plentiful renewable energy, but scientists don't yet know how to control its awesome power.

Nuclear fusion in the Sun's core is what keeps it burning. Here, loops of searing hot plasma are flaring from its surface.

FEELING THE FORCE

Forces are pushing and pulling around you all the time, although you might not always realize they're there. Right now, forces are helping to hold your body together and keeping it on the ground.

Forces at large

Forces are ways in which things affect each other. Sometimes you can see what forces do, like the force of a bat hitting a ball, but some work on levels only scientists can observe. Physical forces, the type that can be seen in the world around you, work in pairs. For instance, if something pushes forward, there must be a force pushing backward too. When you're standing on the ground, the Earth is actually pushing up with the same force.

Rockets are powered by pairs of forces. Jets of super-powerful exhaust gas shoot backward out of the rocket, propelling it upward at the same time.

Keep on moving

Objects tend to resist changes in movement. This means that you need a force to start something moving, and it then continues to move unless another force affects it. In theory, this tendency, called inertia, should keep a moving object going forever, but everyone knows that perpetual motion like this doesn't happen. That's because of a force called friction, which is created when surfaces rub together. For centuries, inventors tried to build perpetual motion machines, but friction makes it impossible on Earth.

Dolphins have smooth, sleek bodies to overcome friction in water.

Objects in space can keep moving because there's no air, so no friction.

42

The fantastic four

Forces also exist on much tinier and more immense scales than the pushes and pulls between everyday objects. Physicists think there are four fundamental forces which define how matter, and the universe itself, is held together.

Gravitational force keeps the Earth in orbit around the Sun.

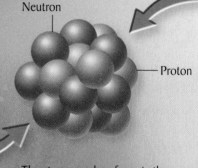

Gravitational force is an attraction between two objects. It's very weak – a trillion trillion times weaker than the strong nuclear force – but has an infinite range.

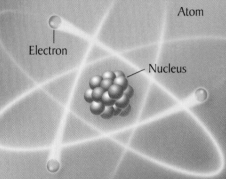

Atom

Electron

Nucleus

Neutron

Neutron

Proton

The electromagnetic or EM force controls the way that any particle with an electrical charge behaves. It's also responsible for magnetism and light waves, and holds together the electrons and nucleus of an atom.

The weak nuclear force allows particles inside atoms to break down over time. This diagram shows a neutron breaking down into three smaller particles.

The strong nuclear force is the strongest force in nature, but it only works on an atomic scale. It tightly binds together the protons and neutrons in an atom's nucleus.

Life without forces

The fundamental forces are so important, a universe without them would be hard to imagine. For a start, matter couldn't exist. Protons naturally repel each other, so without the strong nuclear force to hold them together, the nucleus of every atom would blow apart like a nuclear bomb. The EM force is also essential, keeping every atom's electrons in place – otherwise the universe would be an infinite soup of random particles.

INTERNET LINK
For a link to a website where you can play a game demonstrating the power of the four forces, go to **www.usborne-quicklinks.com**

The weak nuclear force allows radioactive decay and nuclear fusion to take place. Since the Sun is fuelled by this process, without the weak force it would stop burning. Darkness would cover the Earth, and life as we know it would fizzle out.

GRIPPING GRAVITY

If you jump up into the air, just a little or as high as you can, you'll always fall back to the ground. Your body is pulled toward the Earth by a mysterious force called gravity.

Pulling together

Gravity is a force that attracts things to each other. The bigger something is, the stronger its gravitational force. Earth is massive, so its gravity is strong enough to attract everything on its surface toward it. But even small things, like your hand and this book, have a force of gravity attracting them together. It's just too weak to feel.

The smaller the object, the weaker its gravity. The Moon is one-sixth the size of the Earth, so astronauts leap around easily in its weak gravity.

A planet larger than Earth would have stronger gravity. An astronaut on its surface would find it hard to stand, never mind leap.

Weight watching

Everything that's made of something has mass, and everything that has mass also has a weight when it's being affected by gravity. The weight depends on the mass of the objects involved, and the distance between their centers of gravity. Earth's center of gravity is literally in its center, and yours is roughly around your navel. The farther apart these two things are, the less you weigh, although the change is very slight.

Black holes

A black hole is the remains of a star that has collapsed in on itself, creating an unimaginably powerful gravitational pull. A black hole's gravity is so strong that nothing can escape from it, not even light, so it can't actually be seen. Some scientists think that in the heart of a black hole, the laws of space and time as we know them no longer exist. In effect, something that's sucked into a black hole disappears from this universe.

This computer image shows a black hole's gravity sucking in matter from all around.

Deeply dippy

No one knows for sure what causes gravity, but many scientists think that it's the way that space and time curve. Time and space are very difficult to imagine, but they're often compared to a huge rubbery sheet, stretching to infinity. Planets and stars are like tennis balls on the sheet, making it sag where they lie. Everything around them that's near enough will be pulled toward the dip they make. That's how a planet's gravity pulls things toward it.

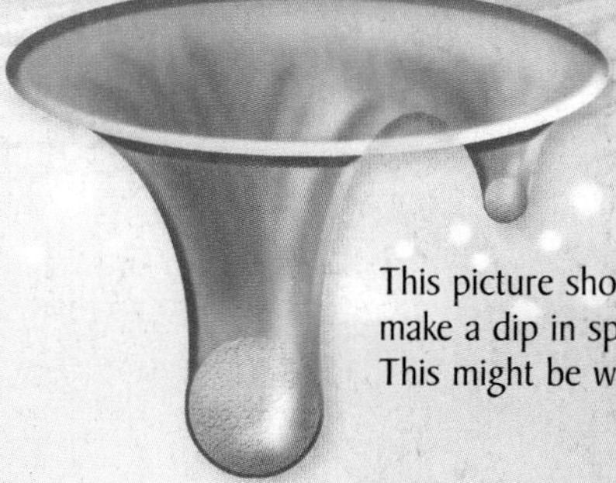

This picture shows how planets make a dip in space and time. This might be what creates gravity.

As soon as they jump from their plane, gravity pulls these skydivers back down to Earth. They weigh slightly less in the air than on the ground, because they're farther from the Earth's center.

INTERNET LINK
For a link to a website where you can take a trip inside a black hole, go to www.usborne-quicklinks.com

TRAVELS IN TIME

W̲hat's the time? By now, it's already a few seconds later than when you started reading this page. Everyone knows that time exists and can be measured, but the way it behaves is more bizarre than you might think.

Albert Einstein's theories on space and time revolutionized people's understanding of the strange ways in which these things work.

The fourth dimension

The famous physicist Albert Einstein created a theory that time is another dimension that exists alongside the three dimensions of space around you. Together, he called these four dimensions "spacetime." It is possible to move in any direction in the three dimensions you can see, but you can move only one way through time.

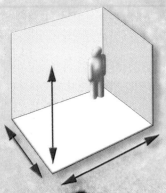

Space as you see it has three dimensions: up and down, forward and back, and side to side. You can move in any of these directions.

Time is the fourth dimension, which you can only move through forward. With a clock or watch you can measure how far through time you've traveled.

The flow of time

Any clock will tell you that, say, sixty seconds pass in every minute, and the length of that minute never varies. But it seems that, in the right conditions, the flow of time can change. For instance, gravity creates "bulges" in the fabric of space and time that affect the way time flows, although you normally can't detect its effects.

How time flies

According to Einstein, time speeds up or slows down depending on how fast you travel, although this only becomes noticeable at extremely high speeds. Imagine you went on a year-long trip around the universe, moving at just below light speed (300,000km or 186,000 miles per second). One year would pass for you, but several would pass on Earth. Since humans can't travel at such speeds, no one has ever directly observed this effect. But mathematical equations show that it must be true.

INTERNET LINK
For a link to a website that demonstrates the strange effects of light-speed travel, go to
www.usborne-quicklinks.com

Time travel: fact or fiction?

Everyone thinks that journeying through time to the past or the future is something that only happens in movies and books. But it might actually be possible, through a wormhole – a tunnel through spacetime linking one point in the universe to another one elsewhere. Unfortunately, scientists don't know if wormholes are real, and even if they are, it would be impossible for anyone to use them. But for now, they're the closest thing to a genuine time machine that humans are aware of.

In theory, wormholes could allow you to travel between any two points in either time or space.

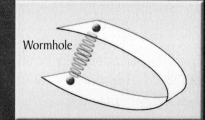

Normally, two points in the vastness of spacetime would be much too far apart to travel between.

Einstein thought that spacetime is curved. If this is true, and most experts believe it is, the distance between the two points could be shorter than it seems.

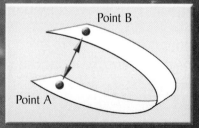

Shortcuts called wormholes would allow you to travel between the two points. Wormholes might exist in the heart of black holes, but there's no way of finding out yet.

UNDER PRESSURE

Pressure is everywhere. Right now, the Earth's atmosphere is pressing on you from all around. There's pressure inside your body, too, helping it to keep its shape.

Getting jiggly

Pressure isn't just things pressing together, it's what happens when molecules jiggle around. The molecules of a gas or liquid in an enclosed space naturally move around. They bounce off the walls of the container, pressing outward in every direction as they do so. If the space becomes more limited, they collide more often and the pressure on the walls increases.

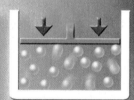

The molecules of gas in a jar move around randomly, bouncing off each other and the container.

If the gas is squeezed into a smaller space, the molecules become closer together and collide more, applying more pressure on the jar's walls.

The heart creates pressure to pump blood around the body. This image shows its intricate, root-like system of vessels, through which the blood flows.

Standing firm

Liquid and gas molecules under pressure can generate enough force to make soft things feel solid. It's pressurized water in plants' stems that makes them stand firm and upright, and pressurized air and blood in our bodies that help to keep us from becoming floppy bags of bones and goo.

Atmospheric pressure

The air in Earth's atmosphere presses on you from every direction with surprising strength. In fact, the weight of air pressing down over one square meter of the Earth is heavier than a large elephant. So why doesn't it crush you? The answer is that the fluids in your body push outward with a force that's equal to the force caused by the air pressure outside it. These two forces cancel each other out.

Hurricanes are fierce, swirling masses of wind, rain and lightning, that form in areas of very low air pressure over the sea. Some, like this one, are huge enough to be photographed from space by satellites.

Pressure and weather

Enormous masses of air constantly rise and fall all over the world, creating areas of low or high air pressure beneath them. We don't see them, but we feel their effects. Pressure changes are the driving force behind most of Earth's weather, especially extreme weather like hurricanes and tornadoes.

A tornado forms when huge differences in air pressure cause air to start spinning in a tight, funnel-shaped formation.

It extends down, causing massive damage when it touches the ground. Tornadoes hurl cars and buildings around like toys.

INTERNET LINK
For a link to a website where you can see the effects of pressure beneath the ocean, go to www.usborne-quicklinks.com

Down in the deep

Like air, water applies pressure to everything it surrounds. Divers have to be specially equipped in the deep sea, as the pressure of water around them could easily crush their lungs. Creatures that live in the ocean depths have a startling way to deal with these extreme conditions. The natural pressure inside their bodies is so high that they literally explode if they're brought to the surface.

This scuba diver is breathing air from pressurized tanks. The air is kept at the same pressure as the surrounding water, so his lungs don't collapse.

GOOD VIBRATIONS

Everyone knows how to make sounds. Try humming: you can hear the noise, but you can probably feel something in your throat too. That's your vocal cords vibrating, and they do that because all sounds are made by vibration.

Making waves

Every sound, from the slightest rustle to the most earsplitting roar, is a wave of energy made up of tiny, vibrating particles. The energy transfers from particle to particle until it reaches your ears. Sound waves can travel through gases, liquids and solids, but not through a vacuum. That's why the emptiness of space is completely silent.

The more high-pitched the sound, the closer together the vibrations are. A sound's frequency (the number of sound waves per second) is measured in Hertz (Hz).

A high-pitched sound, such as a whistle, has a high frequency.

A low-pitched sound, such as a tuba, has a low frequency.

The height of the peaks (tops) and depth of the troughs (bottoms) of a sound wave is its amplitude, which shows how loud it is. Loudness is measured in decibels (dB).

A soft sound has a small amplitude.

A loud sound has a large amplitude.

Blue whales can make noises up to a deafening 188dB, louder than any other living thing. The sound waves can be heard thousands of miles away through the water.

Sound in a hurry

In air, sound waves move at more than 1,000km (621 miles) per hour. A person running at that speed could cross three soccer fields in a second. But sound travels even more speedily in liquids and solids, because their particles are closer together. In fact, sound carries five times more quickly through water than through air, and 15 times more quickly through steel.

INTERNET LINK
For a link to a website where you can listen to whale sounds, go to
www.usborne-quicklinks.com

The speed of sound

Light moves more quickly than sound, which is why you always see lightning before you hear the thunder it makes, never the other way around. If something starts to travel more quickly than the speed of sound (331.3m, or 1087ft, per second), it's said to be going at supersonic speed. As a supersonic aircraft flies, it squashes the air in front. This is released behind the plane as a shock wave, which makes a tremendous boom.

The misty "egg" in this unique image is actually a mass of air molecules being shaken by shock waves behind a supersonic plane. It's incredibly hard to capture this effect, as it only exists for a moment. This picture was taken from an aircraft carrier in the sea.

A resounding success

You may have heard people say that opera singers can shatter a glass just by singing. This is true, but it's not just to do with the loudness of the sound – it's an effect called resonance. Everything in the universe is vibrating just a little, at its own frequency. If a sound wave matches this rate of vibration it causes resonance, making the object vibrate very strongly and maybe even shaking it to pieces.

Sound weapons

Although we don't think of it as being dangerous, sound can make a surprisingly effective weapon. Scientists are developing weapons which fire "sound bullets" of around 140dB. Any sounds over 120dB are painful to humans, so the bullets, which are actually very concentrated sound waves, can easily put their target out of action.

A sound is made in the end of the weapon, and amplified by a series of crystal wafers as it passes through the tube.

Crystal wafer

When it leaves the tube, the sound wave is extremely loud, but the person it's aimed at is the only one who can hear it.

SOUNDS OF SILENCE

What's described as sound is generally only what people can hear. But there's a world of noise around you that you can't hear at all.

INTERNET LINK
For a link to a website with animations and activities about sound waves, echoes and ultrasound, go to **www.usborne-quicklinks.com**

Hidden noise

The sounds that human ears can detect measure between about 20 and 20,000 Hertz. Higher-pitched sounds are called ultrasound, and ones with lower pitches are called infrasound or subsonic sound. Humans can't hear these, but some other creatures can. For instance, elephants take shelter long before a storm starts, because they can detect the low rumble of distant thunder much sooner than humans. They also communicate with infrasound calls.

Here's how the range of sounds humans can detect compares to those of some other creatures.

25,000–100,000Hz – bat squeaks

40,000Hz – upper limit of dogs' hearing

20,000Hz – upper limit of human hearing

300–3,000Hz – human speech

20Hz – lower limit of human hearing

17–20Hz – blue whale calls

12–35Hz – elephant calls

Bouncing sound

When a sound wave bounces off something, it makes an echo – a repeat of the original sound. Certain animals use the echoes from the sounds they make to find their way around, a technique called echo location.

Echoes from bats' high-pitched squeaks tell them where to find tasty moths to eat.

Baby booms

The ability of sound waves to travel through different substances and bounce back can be used to build up pictures of things you can't see or measure easily. Images made by bouncing ultrasound waves are mostly used in hospitals, to look at unborn babies inside their mothers.

Today's ultrasound scanners are so sophisticated, they can show if an unborn baby is smiling or frowning. This baby is curled up and fast asleep.

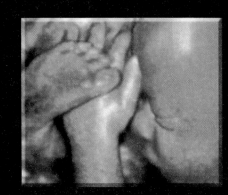

See beneath the sea

Ships use ultrasound waves to find out the depth of the ocean in a particular spot, or to see the seabed's shape. This method, called sonar, can also be used to find shipwrecks in the murky depths.

The computer image below shows ridges and valleys beneath the sea. A ship sends out ultrasound waves and measures how long it takes for them to bounce back from the ocean floor. It takes thousands of sound waves bounced off different spots to make an image like this.

Ghostbusting

Although very low infrasound is beyond the human range of hearing, its vibrations seem to have weird effects. Some places where people claimed to feel the presence of ghosts have turned out to be "haunted" by infrasound, which was tricking their brains into making them feel nervous and afraid.

Infrasound sometimes causes people's vision to become blurry, making them see shadowy, ghost-like shapes.

THE HEAT IS ON

You can't see them moving, but the molecules of all solids, liquids or gases are never still. Heat is energy that passes from the vibrating or spinning molecules of an object to anything cooler.

Molecules on the move

When something is heated, it's said to gain more internal energy, which makes its molecules vibrate more quickly and push each other farther apart. So, most things grow or swell as they're heated, and shrink as they cool down. The Eiffel Tower in Paris, France, is actually 15cm (5.9in) taller on the hottest days of the year, because it expands in the sun.

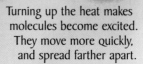

Turning up the heat makes molecules become excited. They move more quickly, and spread farther apart.

When a substance cools down, its molecules start to vibrate more slowly, moving closer together.

Feeling the heat

Heat is always on the move between hotter and cooler areas, and it has three different ways of getting around. It spreads outward as infrared radiation, invisible waves given out by every object in the universe. It travels from one part of a substance to another part by conduction: metals conduct heat well, but the best conductor of all is diamond. In air and liquid, heat spreads by convection, which makes it rise and sink in a constant loop.

Heat at the bottom of this lava lamp causes molecules of solid wax to spread out, turning the wax into a liquid. Convection makes the wax flow up, then down, the lamp.

Seeing with heat

Pictures taken by infrared cameras, like this one of a baboon, show patterns of color based on an object's hot and cold areas. Since infrared cameras can "see" heat, they can detect objects that are hidden behind or inside something else, or in complete darkness. They can also show us details that normal light alone wouldn't reveal.

Letting off steam

If you make a liquid hot enough, it starts to boil – that is, it turns into a gas. Normally, water bubbles and turns to steam as it boils, and this energy loss keeps it from getting any hotter. But if for some reason bubbles can't form, the water's temperature rises and rises until it's beyond the normal boiling temperature, and it becomes superheated. If something acts as a trigger, all the stored heat energy is unleashed in one huge burst. In some parts of the world, the power of superheating has created explosive columns of water called geysers.

INTERNET LINK
For a link to a website with surprising infrared images and infrared facts, go to **www.usborne-quicklinks.com**

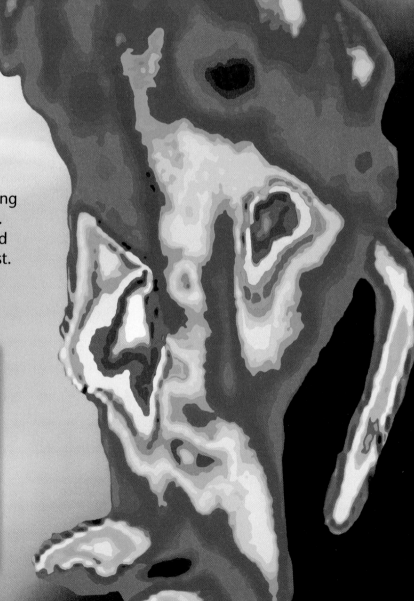

Infrared imaging displays this baboon's hottest parts in red and yellow, and her coolest areas in blue and purple. Normally, you could only learn information like this by touch.

The geysers in this photograph show superheating's mighty force. Water in underground chambers is superheated by hot rock surrounding it, before erupting in violent, boiling sprays.

COLD SCIENCE

If you have a freezer in your home, you'll know it's useful to be able to cool things down. But what about if you make them colder still? Just how cold can something get, and what happens to it?

This scientist is studying a preserved brain. No one has done it yet, but it's thought that one day it might be possible to keep frozen brains alive, then transplant them.

Feeling the cold

Really low temperatures can be both helpful and harmful to living things. Extreme cold normally kills living cells and tissue, but under the right conditions, it can be used to preserve them. For instance, blood and body organs can be kept in a laboratory in very cold liquid nitrogen, then thawed and used in operations.

Frozen life isn't confined to a lab, though. Some animals have a high level of a natural antifreeze called glycol inside them that allows their bodies to chill completely and become death-like during the winter. In spring, they thaw out and wake up as if they'd simply been taking a nap.

Wood frogs hibernate during the harsh winter. They bury themselves in icy pond mud, and their bodies freeze solid.

Freezing would kill most animals, but the frogs' unique body chemistry allows them to revive in the spring with no ill effects.

How low can you go?

The lowest naturally occurring temperature recorded on Earth is -89°C (-128°F), in the Antarctic. That's extremely cold, although not nearly the coldest temperature in the universe. One of Neptune's moons, Triton, has a surface temperature of a chilling -235°C (-455°F), but even that isn't the coldest known place. Radiation left behind from its creation allowed scientists to measure the overall temperature of the universe itself – an astonishing -270.42°C (-518.76°F). That's almost as cold as you can possibly get.

Absolutely freezing

The lowest theoretical temperature that could exist is -273.15°C (-523.67°F), also known as absolute zero. Something cooled to this level can't get any colder, because its internal energy is at a minimum. Scientists think that reaching absolute zero might be impossible, although they have cooled atoms to within a millionth of a degree of it using laser pulses to slow down their movement.

Laser beams apply a very tiny force to any atoms they touch. If you shine lasers on an atom from many different angles, it can be made to move more slowly. No one has yet stopped an atom completely, though.

That's super cool!

Helium gas cooled to about -269°C (-516°F) turns to a liquid. But at a few fractions of a degree above absolute zero, it becomes something called a superfluid. Superfluids are unique because all their atoms travel at the same speed and in the same direction, instead of randomly as in normal liquids. This makes superfluids incredibly smooth-flowing: they can move without friction through the tiniest of gaps, and even up the sides of containers.

INTERNET LINK
For a link to a website where you can see what happens to atoms at low temperatures, go to www.usborne-quicklinks.com

Superconductors

At around -253°C (-423°F), some materials become superconductors, which means they allow electricity to pass freely through them without resistance. So, unlike normal conductors, they waste no energy as heat while current flows through them. In fact, they can conduct electric current for years with next to no energy loss. They also produce exceptionally powerful magnetic fields.

Electric current flows easily through superconducting materials like this, creating a magnetic field strong enough to make a metal disk float above it. The glowing mist is liquid nitrogen, which keeps the material cool enough to be a superconductor.

CURRENT AFFAIRS

You probably know already that electricity has the power to light a room, make a TV work, and so on. But you might not know that this power exists inside everything.

Feeling energetic

People often describe electricity as energy, but that's not quite right: actually, electricity carries energy. Energy from electricity can be gained or lost. For instance, it is lost when a lightbulb changes it into light and heat. But while this conversion is going on, electricity still continues to flow through the wire. So, the energy and the electricity itself must be separate things.

This lightbulb turns electrical energy into light and heat energy.

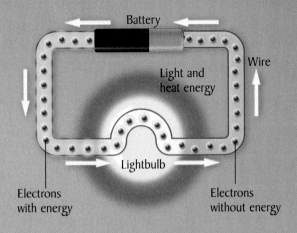

If you connect a battery and a lightbulb with a loop of wire, you've made an electrical circuit. Electricity flows through the circuit and the bulb uses the energy it carries.

Electrifying atoms

The answer to what electricity really is lies inside an atom, where protons and electrons hold positive and negative electrical charges. Normally there is the same amount of each, but if atoms lose or gain electrons, they can become positively or negatively charged (and are called ions).

Electricity is a result of the way that charged particles behave. Because they are charged, there is an electric force between them. Any charge produces an invisible effect around it called an electric field. Another charge that strays into this field feels an electric force.

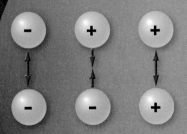

Electrical fields cause charged particles to push and pull. Those with the same charge repel each other; those with opposite charges are attracted.

Charging ahead

Charges on the move are called electrical current, and this is what carries electrical energy through a wire. An electrical current always needs something to flow through, and something to move it. Batteries, for instance, act like pumps to move charges along.

Charges move very slowly: in fact, sometimes they don't travel at all, they just jiggle around. So how can a light come on right away when you flip a switch? It's because there are already charged atoms in the wires between the switch and the bulb. Think of the current working in the same way as a wheel – if you give it a push, the whole thing is instantly affected. You don't have to wait for the movement to travel from one part of the wheel to another.

Electricity flows with no resistance through the bundles of wire in superconducting cables like this one, so no energy is wasted.

Good conduct

A substance that allows charge to move through it easily is called a conductor. Metals are really good conductors, but materials like wood and plastic barely conduct at all. Whether something conducts or not is all to do with the properties of its electrons and the way they can or can't move.

INTERNET LINK
For a link to a website with interactive animations about electricity, circuits and more, go to www.usborne-quicklinks.com

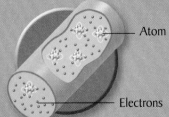

Atom

Electrons

A conductor is like a pipe full of water. The current flows freely between atoms in a moving "sea" of electrons.

An insulator is like a pipe full of ice. Its electrons are fixed in place, so current can barely flow.

Meeting resistance

Almost every substance, even a conductor, has a little resistance to electricity flowing through it. Resistance causes energy to be lost – in fact, about 10% of electrical energy is wasted as it flows through wires, usually as heat. Resistance isn't all bad, though, as it's what allows electric fires and toasters to work.

TAKING CHARGE

When electrical charges flow, they make an electric current. But if they have nowhere to go to, they build up instead. Eventually, they may be unleashed as a powerful spark.

Building up charge

Normally, a material's atoms are electrically neutral, which means that they have equal positive and negative electrical charges. But if you rub together two insulators (materials that don't conduct electricity well), some electrons will be transferred from one to the other, making one negative and the other positive. This build-up of charge is called static electricity, and the energy stored by separating this charge is measured by voltage: the greater the amount of charge separated, the greater the voltage.

A spark of static electricity can jump between any two objects with opposite charges – in this case, the tips of a pair of nails.

Electric body

Static electricity is what you sometimes experience if your feet build up charge as you walk across a carpeted room then touch a metal doorknob. As the charge from your body leaps to the doorknob, you may hear a crackling sound and even see a spark. This can be up to several thousand volts, but you rarely feel more than a sting.

Static cling

If static can exist between any insulators in contact with each other, you might wonder why you don't see sparks every time you pick up a book or a pencil. In fact, the amount of charge depends on the materials and the amount of touching surface area between them. The flatter the objects, the more surface contact, and the more the voltage increases.

Some materials give up electrons and become charged more readily than others. For instance, hair gives up electrons easily, and plastic is better at gaining them.

Using a plastic comb to bend water may look like magic, but it's easy if you run the comb through your hair first. This charges the comb with electrons, and the water is then attracted to the comb's negative charge.

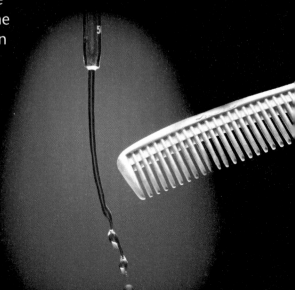

Sparks in the sky

Lightning is the big, bold brother of the spark that jumps between your hand and a doorknob, and, like your skin and the knob, it's caused by an attraction between oppositely charged things. If ice and rain rub together in a cloud, they create a build-up of separated charges in the cloud's top and bottom. The negative charges in the bottom are attracted to positive charges in the ground, and electrons start to flow between the two, creating a path through the sky. This path is what lightning leaps along.

A model plane is being used to test how real aircraft react to lightning strikes. This "lightning" is a high-voltage spark, generated in a lab.

INTERNET LINK
For a link to a website where you can watch animations about lightning, circuits and electricity, go to www.usborne-quicklinks.com

Sprites and jets

Every so often, lightning is generated from the upper part of a storm cloud instead of the lower part, and its unusually intense electrical field creates a spectacular light show. It might appear as a massive, jellyfish-shaped burst of red light called a sprite, which shoots up into the air high above the storm, or as a jet – a flash of blue light spreading upward at up to 100km (62 miles) per second. But very few people have seen or photographed these rare, unpredictable sights, because they happen so far up.

Lightning in the lab

In the late 19th century, a scientist named Nikola Tesla revolutionized the way people thought about and used electricity. One of his many electrical creations was a device to harness the extreme power of lightning inside a laboratory. He named his invention, which transforms opposite charges into brief pulses of powerful electricity, a Tesla coil.

Here, a scientist sees the shocking effects of a Tesla coil. Although he looks worried, he is protected by a Faraday cage, a metal suit designed to keep bolts of electricity away from whatever's inside it.

THE BODY ELECTRIC

In the story of Frankenstein, a monster was brought
to life with electricity. But that's not as far-fetched as
it sounds – electricity in our bodies is what allows us
to move, think and react to the world around us.

Human computers

In a way, people are like living computers – they use
electricity to sort complex information and react to
instructions from outside. Everything you sense is translated
into electrical signals that travel between your body parts
and your brain. The tiny cells which your body is made
of act like batteries, generating electricity as charged
atoms, called ions, move through them.

Brains and chips

The brain is more complex than
the most sophisticated machine on
Earth. Inside it, over 10 billion nerve
cells, called neurons, are constantly
exchanging information. Scientists
have recently created an electronic
"neuro-chip," a computer chip
which strengthens the pulses of
electricity from neurons and
transfers them to a computer for
processing. This will improve
scientists' knowledge of how the
brain works, making it easier
to treat brain diseases.

Here you can see a nerve
cell that's been grown on
an electronic sensor chip.
Each chip is only about the
size of a pinhead, but can
record huge amounts of
information about how
nerves respond
to things.

Keeping pace

Have you ever wondered what keeps your heart beating? It's a series of regular electrical jolts from a tiny clump of cells inside your heart called pacemakers. They often die or wear out with age, but their owner can be given a new lease on life by being fitted with an artificial electrical pacemaker. The batteries need changing every ten or so years, though, and can be damaged easily by strong magnetic fields.

Recently, scientists have found a way to change the flow of substances in and out of the heart's cells by adding a chemical instruction called a gene. The altered flow creates a negative electrical charge in the heart's ordinary cells, turning them into new pacemaker cells.

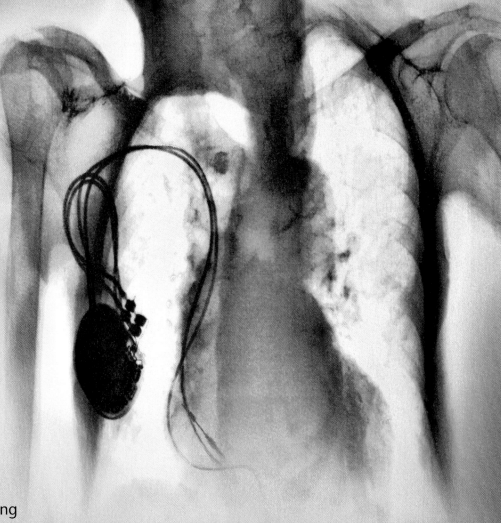

This X-ray image shows an electronic pacemaker keeping a person's heartbeat regular. Scientists are finding new ways to repair the heart's cells to make bulky implants like this a thing of the past.

INTERNET LINK
For a link to a website where you can take a 3-D tour of a brain, go to www.usborne-quicklinks.com

Chain of command

Just as a computer reacts when you click on a mouse button, your body can translate actions into responses. The central nervous system, made of your brain and spinal cord, interprets information from your senses and sends commands through chains of neurons. And, just like a computer, it runs on electricity.

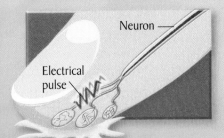

When a neuron is excited by sensations such as touch, it generates a tiny electrical pulse. At the same time, chemicals called neurotransmitters are released in the cell.

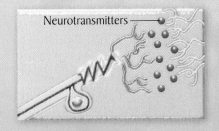

The electrical pulse travels through the body to the neuron's thin, finger-like ends, in the spinal cord. All neurons almost, but not quite, touch the ends of the next one.

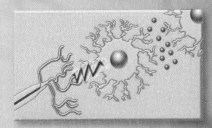

The neurotransmitters help the pulse to jump to the next neuron. This neuron then passes the pulse on to another, until the message reaches the brain.

MIGHTY MAGNETS

Magnetism is an invisible force which certain materials can create, and which most things are affected by. Planet Earth is a magnet, and you're magnetic too.

Here, magnetic powder is being used to dust for fingerprints. Some of the powder sticks to grease in the prints, and the rest is lifted away by a magnet.

Pole position

A free-moving magnet always swivels to point in a north-south direction. The parts of a magnet that control this attraction are its north and south poles. Even if you cut a magnet into many pieces, each one will have two poles.

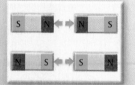

Identical magnetic poles always push each other away.

Opposite magnetic poles always pull each other together.

Getting magnetic

If you've ever tried sticking something to a refrigerator door, you'll know that some things are magnetic and some aren't. A magnet is anything with its own magnetic field – a force that affects other magnetic things around it. Every molecule of a magnet is like a tiny magnet itself, and all its poles point the same way. Some materials, such as iron, can become magnets for a short time when placed in a magnetic field, which makes the magnetic poles inside them line up together.

Iron filings scattered around a magnet always line up in the shape of its magnetic field, as this picture shows.

INTERNET LINK
For a link to a website where you can
take a virtual tour of an MRI machine,
go to www.usborne-quicklinks.com

Magnetic Earth

The center of the Earth is made of solid iron surrounded by a layer of liquid iron. As the Earth spins, this fluid metal swirls and generates a magnetic field around the planet, making it act like a giant magnetic bar. A compass needle always points north because its poles are attracted to the poles of the Earth's magnetic field.

Some animals have tiny crystals of a magnetic substance called magnetite inside their bodies, so they can detect the Earth's magnetic field. This astonishing "sixth sense" acts like a natural compass, guiding animals around the world on journeys of thousands of miles to have babies or find food.

Living magnets

When you think of magnets, you usually think of metals. But solid things with lots of water in them, including animals and humans, can be magnetic too. Water is diamagnetic, which means the electrons in its atoms, which all have their own magnetic fields, always repel magnetism from outside. Although the diamagnetic force is about 100,000 times weaker than normal magnetism, if you have a strong enough magnetic field you can use diamagnetism to make living things float.

Seeing with magnets

MRI (magnetic resonance imaging) is a way of using magnets to see inside the body. The patient lies in a tube that gives out a powerful magnetic field, and radio waves are passed through the body. This causes some of the patient's body atoms to change their movement. Only about three in every million atoms are affected, but that's enough information for a computer to generate amazing, detailed images.

This MRI scan of a brain has revealed a tumor on the left side.

If a frog is placed in a tube with a strong magnetic field, the electrons in the frog's atoms will try to push against the outside force.

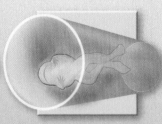
The frog will start to float as its charged electrons repel the surrounding magnetic field. Even a human could float in a strong enough field.

65

ELECTROMAGNETISM

You might think from its name alone that electromagnetism has something to do with electricity and magnetism, and you'd be absolutely right. They have many features in common, which is why they're often described together as a single force.

A versatile force

Electromagnetism is one of the most important forces in the universe. As well as controlling how electricity and magnetism work, it holds together the atoms that everything is made of.

You'll also see the word "electromagnetic" used to describe some types of rays. That's because the tiny blips of electromagnetic energy known as photons are also what make rays of light, microwaves, and the whole range of energy waves known as the electromagnetic spectrum.

Electromagnetic forces inside atoms create contact forces. These keep objects from merging together, for example, stopping the atoms in this hand from merging with the surface it's touching.

Electrons whizz around an atom's nucleus (middle) in areas known as shells. The farther from the nucleus an electron's shell is, the more energy it has. Electrons can move from shell to shell, gaining or losing energy as they go. The energy exists in little "packets" called photons.

If an electron moves closer to the nucleus, as in this diagram, it loses energy and gives out a photon. An electron moves to an outer shell when it gains energy from a photon. These moving photons are electromagnetic waves.

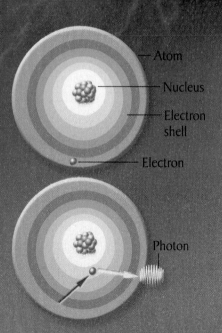

- Atom
- Nucleus
- Electron shell
- Electron
- Photon

Making contact

The atoms that make up all objects are mostly empty space, so what keeps two things from merging together when they touch? The answer is electromagnetism. Electromagnetic (EM) forces cause electrons in an atom's outer shell to repel electrons in other atoms. This creates an invisible barrier between solid things which we experience as their hard surface.

Let's stick together

Electromagnetic forces don't just keep solid things solid, they also play a vital part in joining atoms together to make molecules. Usually, an atom has an equal number of positive protons and negative electrons, which means the charges are balanced, making the atom electrically neutral. Since all the charges are canceled out, in theory it shouldn't be possible for atoms to attract each other and form molecules. But when atoms get close enough, the EM force allows this to happen.

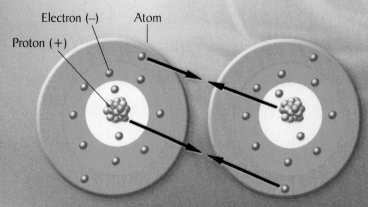

The electromagnetic force allows the negatively charged electrons of one atom to attract the positively charged protons of another, so the atoms can stick together.

Making magnets

Since electricity and magnetism are so closely linked, you can use one to create the other. Coiled wire with an electric current running through it generates a magnetic field, and if you put materials such as iron in the coils, they become electromagnets – magnets you can turn on and off by changing the current. These are used in all kinds of gadgets, such as phones and modems, and also to create extra-smooth movement. Scientists are developing ways to launch spacecraft more easily using maglev (**mag**netic **lev**itation) tracks, which avoid the slowing effect of friction by making the rocket float.

When the coils in this electromagnetic launch track are electrified, they generate a powerful magnetic field, shown in red in this computer image. The field repels magnets underneath the rocket and it floats above the track, allowing for a smoother, faster launch.

INTERNET LINK
For a link to a website with electromagnet activities, go to www.usborne-quicklinks.com

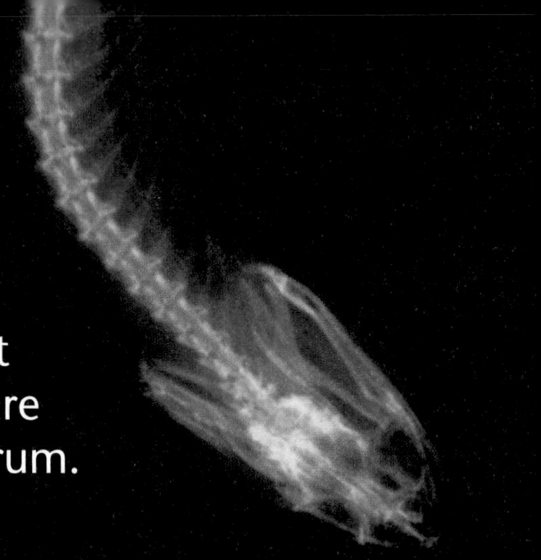

INVISIBLE LIGHT

The whole universe is tingling with energy waves. Light is a group of energy waves you can see, but it is actually one part of a great range of waves that are invisible, known as the electromagnetic (EM) spectrum.

Electromagnetic waves

All EM waves zip through space at the speed of light. Like sound waves, EM waves can travel through solids, liquids and gases, but they can pass through the empty space of a vacuum too. The diagram below shows how EM waves can be grouped by their wavelength, that is, the distance between the top of one wave and the next, and their frequency, which is how many waves pass by in a second.

Gamma rays and X-rays have a short wavelength and high frequency.

The electromagnetic spectrum

- Gamma rays
- X-rays
- UV light
- Visible light
- Infrared light
- Microwaves
- Radio waves

Microwaves and radio waves have a long wavelength and low frequency.

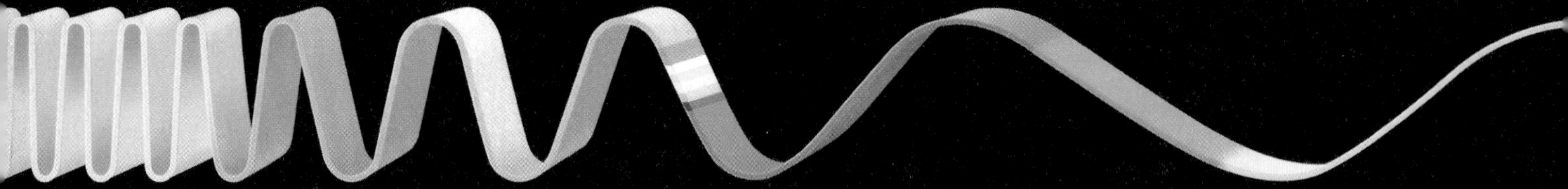

World wide waves

These mysterious glowing shapes are the Large Magellanic Cloud, which lies thousands of light years away in space. Like many space objects, this galaxy gives off radio waves. These are the longest EM waves, whose wavelength makes them good at piercing our cloudy atmosphere. Astronomers use huge, dish-shaped antennas to detect radio waves that come to Earth from space, and they use the information to build up pictures like this one. Radio waves are also widely used for sending TV, radio and mobile phone signals around the world.

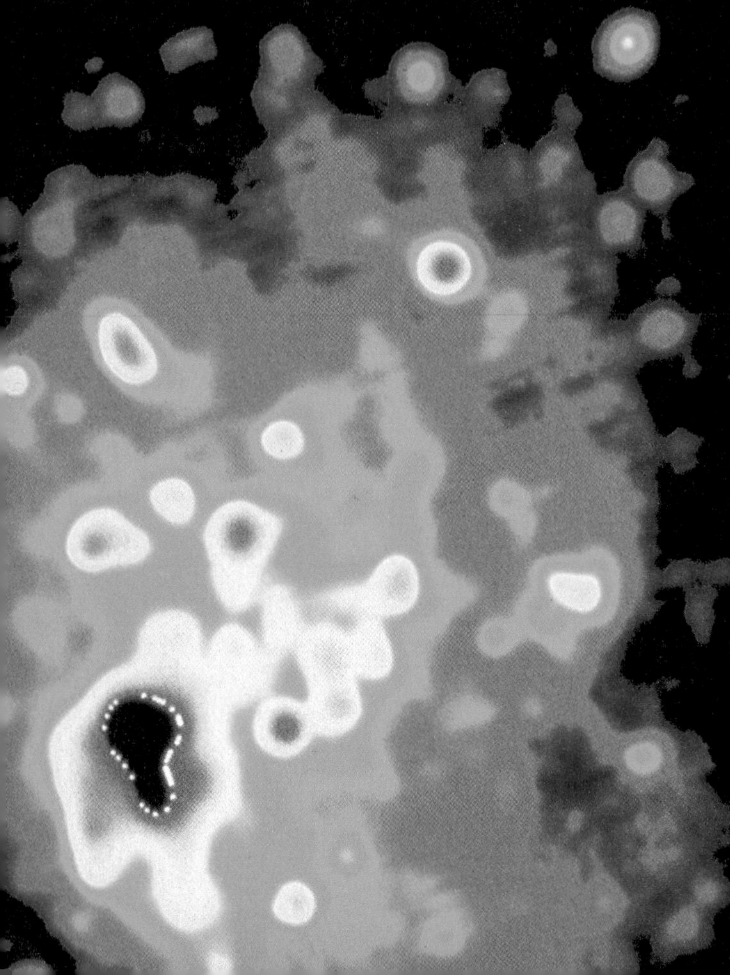

Radio signals from space are turned into images, like this one of a galaxy called the Large Magellanic Cloud.

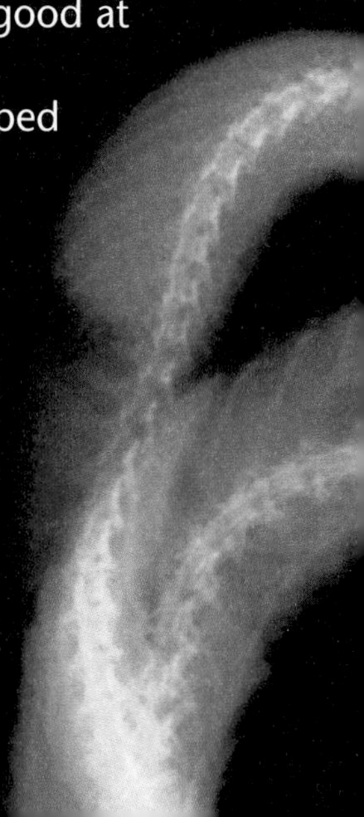

Microwave meals

When you warm up your lunch in a microwave oven, you are using EM waves. Microwaves, like all EM waves, are made of quick-changing electric and magnetic fields. As the fields switch direction, water molecules in the food absorb their energy and spin around like the magnetic needle on a compass. As its molecules move more and more quickly, the food heats up, and cooks.

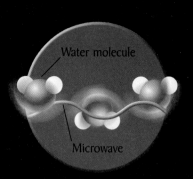

Intense microwaves make water molecules in food spin around millions of times every second.

X-ray vision

X-rays can show views that usually can't be seen. These short, high-energy EM waves can easily pass through some materials that block out light. In X-ray photos, like this one of a snake, the X-rays beam through skin and flesh as effortlessly as light through a window, but bone is dense enough to block them, so it shows up as white.

This portrait is thought to have been painted by the Italian artist Giorgione.

This X-ray photo of the portrait shows a hand that has been painted over.

INTERNET LINK
For a link to a website where you can take a guided tour of the electromagnetic spectrum, go to www.usborne-quicklinks.com

This X-ray photo shows a snake that had a frog for dinner. The X-rays even pass through the frog, showing us the shape of its bones. Bone contains a metal called calcium which soaks up X-rays. This is why the bones show up as solid areas in the photograph.

THE LIGHT FANTASTIC

Light is a form of traveling energy that can be seen. Many of the things that are known about light come from watching the strange or spectacular effects it produces.

Shadow play

Light travels so quickly that you can't see it moving at all. We know it does move, though, because its movement can be blocked. Objects block light by soaking up its energy, or reflecting it back.

Where light is blocked, a shadow forms behind the object blocking it. The more light that is blocked, the darker the shadow that appears.

Light travels in straight lines called rays. You can sometimes see this when sunbeams stream through clouds, or into a dusty room.

This spectacular sight is a total eclipse of the Sun, when the Moon passes in front of the Sun, blocking out its light. The white glow is a super-hot layer of gas that surrounds the Sun, called the corona.

Bouncing back

Most objects reflect some or all of the light rays hitting them. Dark objects soak up most of the light that hits them, but mirrors and white objects reflect back almost all of it. Mirrors are extremely smooth, so light rays that hit them bounce straight back to the viewer, reflecting an image. On a microscopic scale, white surfaces are much rougher, so the reflected light rays are scattered, and no image is seen.

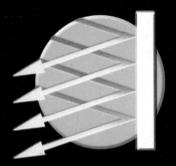

Mirrors reflect light rays straight back to the viewer.

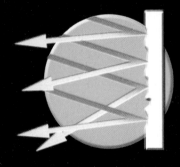

White objects scatter light rays in many directions.

Lightning speed

Thunder is the sound made by lightning, but it often takes a few seconds to hear the thunder after the lightning, even though they happen at the same time. This shows how much more quickly light travels than sound. In fact, light is the fastest thing we know: it moves at 300,000km (186,000 miles) per second through empty space. A ray of light could circle the Earth seven-and-a-half times in a second.

Light takes next to no time to travel 1km, but sound takes three seconds. To find a storm's distance (in km) count the seconds from lightning to thunder and divide by three (for miles, divide by five).

Bending light

Substances that block light are called opaque. Others, like glass or water, are transparent: they let light through. Substances that let some light through are called translucent.

Scientists study the way light moves through substances to learn more about it. When light moves from air into a denser substance, such as glass or water, it slows down. If it hits the substance at an angle it also changes direction. This is why objects seen through water look distorted, or seem closer than they really are.

Insect appears to be here

Insect in the line of fire

Archer fish hunt insects they spot above the water. They know that their line of sight is distorted if they view their prey from an angle, and have developed a trick to make up for it...

The archer fish swims beneath its prey so that its line of sight is true. It then spits a jet of water, knocking the unlucky insect off its perch. Then it's lunchtime.

As light shines through these glass prisms, it changes direction, and splits up into the colors you can see here.

INTERNET LINK

For a link to an animated website with loads of light facts and activities, go to **www.usborne-quicklinks.com**

MAKING LIGHT WORK

Light can do more than let you see: scientists have harnessed its great speed to send messages around the world in the blink of an eye, and have focused its energy in the power and precision of laser beams.

Light messenger

When you're sending an email, or chatting with a friend on the other side of the world, the chances are that your message is being carried by fiber-optic cables. Fiber-optic cables send messages coded as pulses of light. The light is fired by a laser and carried along the inside of incredibly pure strands of glass or plastic called optical fibers.

Fiber-optic cables contain thousands of optical fibers, thinner than a hair, yet stronger than steel. Compared to copper wires, fiber-optics last longer, can carry many more phone calls, and aren't affected by electricity, so you can't get a "crossed wire".

Light travels in straight lines. To keep it moving along through a bending fiber, it's bounced off a mirror-like layer of cladding.

These glowing strands are optical fibers. A single fiber can carry a million phone calls at once, in the form of pulses of light.

Laser light

The shining surfer below is showing off just one of the many uses of lasers. White light is a mixture of colored wavelengths spreading out in many directions. Lasers produce bright beams of a single color, focused in one direction.

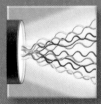

The colored wavelengths in white light spread out in many directions.

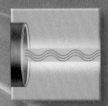

Laser light is focused into one intense, bright wave of a single color.

Lasers are often used in light shows to "paint" pictures on a screen or wall of mist. A computer controls where the beams are fired, and they move so quickly that their tips blur into lines.

INTERNET LINK
For a link to an animated website that shows you all about lasers, go to www.usborne-quicklinks.com

Straight to the point

The narrowness of laser beams suits them to very precise work. In a CD player, a laser scans thousands of microscopic bumps on the underside of a CD, and electronics turn this information into music. Powerful lasers are used in surgery to act as precise cutting instruments, or to weld human tissue together.

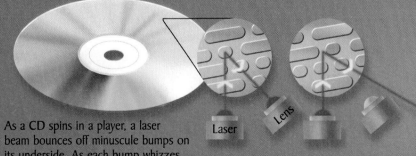

As a CD spins in a player, a laser beam bounces off minuscule bumps on its underside. As each bump whizzes by, a lens picks up a laser signal. The signals are then translated into music.

Laser

Lens

Bump: the lens receives a signal.

No bump: no signal is received.

COLOR

Whether you're painting a picture or choosing a new toothbrush it's easy to take color for granted. The way you see color involves the movement of light, the chemicals in an object and the way your eyes and brain work.

Light reflecting from this macaw's feathers carries its dazzling colors to your eyes.

Rainbows show the colors hidden in sunlight. You only see them when the Sun is behind you.

INTERNET LINK
For a link to a website where you can mix colors online, go to
www.usborne-quicklinks.com

Hidden in sunlight

Rainbows are seen when rays of sunlight shine through raindrops, split up and spread out. They show that light, though it looks white, is really a mixture of differently colored light. These colors are called the visible spectrum. Sometimes the rays also reflect inside the raindrops, producing a second, fainter, rainbow above the first.

Chemical color

Most objects contain chemicals called pigments, which soak up some of the colors from white light as it hits them. The remaining colors are reflected back to your eyes, and these are the colors you see.

A red feather has pigment which soaks up all the colors in light except red, so only red light reaches your eyes.

74

The mind's eye

Both your eyes and your brain are vital to seeing color. Inside the back of your eye are thousands of tiny light-sensitive cells called rods and cones. Rods sense the brightness of light and cones sense its color. There are three types of cones, sensing red, green or blue light, and all colors are seen as mixtures of these three colors. When you look at something, the rods send messages along the optic nerve to tell the brain how bright the object is. The cones send messages about its color. The brain combines these messages to create an image of what you see.

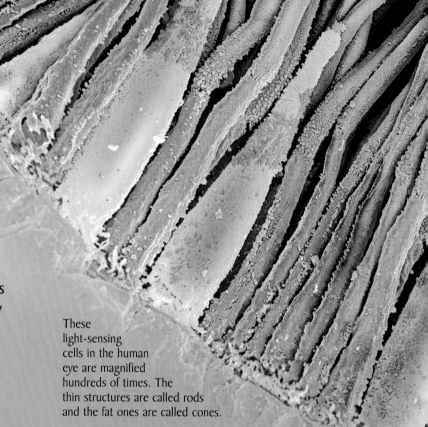

These light-sensing cells in the human eye are magnified hundreds of times. The thin structures are called rods and the fat ones are called cones.

Color film

Not all color is made by pigment. Soap bubbles have a fine double film of oil on their surfaces that splits white light into the colors of the rainbow. These colors reflect off the oil films and interfere with each other. Some colors add together, becoming brighter; others are canceled out, leaving dark areas.

The colors that swim across bubbles are created as light reflects off oil swirling on their surfaces.

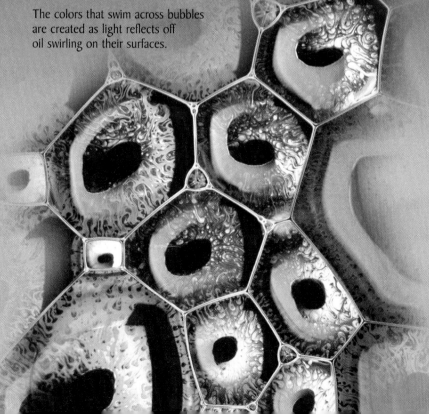

In a different light

Some animals can see colors that can't be seen by humans. Many insects, birds, fish and reptiles can see beyond the violet end of the visible spectrum, into the ultraviolet (UV). Many fruits that look dark to us, such as plums, look bright and inviting in UV, so birds and insects are attracted to them among the much darker-looking leaves.

To human eyes, these silverweed flowers are yellow with no patterns or markings.

To bees, the same flowers have bright UV markings. The patterns lead the bees to the sweet-tasting nectar in the middle of the flower.

OPTICAL ILLUSIONS

You can't always trust your eyes to show you the truth. Optical illusions are visual tricks that surprise your eyes and brains by showing them sights they are unlikely to see in the real world.

Double take

The eyes may see something, but it takes the brain to make sense of what is seen. This is called perception. The pictures on the right can both be perceived in different ways, and this baffles our brains because it wants to decide what it is seeing.

Is this a picture of a vase, or is it two lovers about to kiss?

A young woman looking away or an old lady looking down?

INTERNET LINK
For a link to a website where you can see more optical illusions, and discover how they work, go to **www.usborne-quicklinks.com**

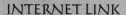

Seeing in stereo

Stereograms use the way the eyes focus on things to create a 3-D illusion. When your eyes focus on a flat page, they both look at the same point and see pretty much the same thing. The brain decides from this that the page is flat. The stereogram on the left repeats a pattern across the page, but it changes slightly each time. These differences fool the brain into thinking it is seeing a 3-D object rather than a flat page, and it joins the patterns together to make a 3-D picture.

To see the hidden 3-D image, let your eyes relax and cross slightly and focus a little way *beyond* the page.

Dizzy spells

The wheels above seem to be spinning – unless you look at a wheel directly. The illusion works because the brain concentrates mainly on what the eyes are focusing on. At the edge of your vision you notice bright things more quickly than dark things, so you see the light parts of the wheels first. This delay creates an illusion of movement from dark to light areas.

The only cogs turning are in your brain... If the illusion above makes you feel dizzy or unwell, please turn to another page.

Sometimes there is a gap between seeing and perceiving, but once the brain has made up its mind it tends to stick with its decision. At first, the picture above may look like a jumble of spots, but it soon becomes very hard *not* to see a dalmatian dog sniffing the ground.

Squares A and B are really the same color. Go to *www.usborne-quicklinks.com* to see the proof. The brain has different areas to deal with perceiving color and shade. Here, the brain is busier working out the color of square B than its exact shade.

These squares seem to bulge but their edges line up straight. The way the smaller squares are arranged makes the corner angles of the larger squares seem sharper than they are, so their edges look slanted.

COMPUTERS EVERYWHERE

Scientists are constantly developing faster and smarter computers. The computers of the future will be built into houses, cars and even clothes. People will be able to use them wherever they go.

Fast worker

A super-fast computer has been developed that uses light, not electricity, to process 8 billion instructions in one second. It contains 256 lasers performing calculations at light-speed and is 1,000 times faster than the computers you use at home or school. The very earliest electronic computers, made in the 1940s, could only process around 5,000 instructions per second.

This laser keyboard can be beamed onto any surface. You can use it like a real keyboard, even though the only thing you touch is a beam of light.

Clip-on computers

Active badges – nametag-sized computers that are pinned onto clothes – can be used as trackers to trace where you are in a building and who you have stopped to talk to. Future badges will also interact with their surroundings in a way that is personalized to you. An automated voice in every room you enter could greet you by name and every computer you sit at could automatically reset itself to your preferences.

INTERNET LINK
For a link to a website about testing new technology, go to www.usborne-quicklinks.com

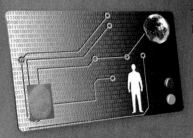

The computers of the future might look like this. As you walk around a building, a computer pinned to your clothes could be storing and sending out information about you.

E-paper

Computerized paper could bring books and magazines to life. It would be flexible and feel like normal paper, but a single page would hold lots of books and articles, illustrated by video clips and animations. Slim, book-sized display panels have already been developed. You can download newspapers and magazines onto them, then fold – or even roll – them up and put them away.

This ultra-thin computer screen folds like a book.

Smartly dressed

Mobile computers already exist in the form of laptops and handhelds, but soon people might be wearing computers on their bodies. "Smart clothing" is made of a type of fabric that combines cloth with computer technology. This could let you make telephone calls from your shirt, or even surf the Internet from your coat.

This small computer screen is attached to the hood of a raincoat. It brings up information about the wearer's surroundings.

Invisible computers

In the future, your life might be monitored by computers that are built into your home, school or office. They would be built in so well that you wouldn't even notice they were there. The computers would determine what you wanted them to do by monitoring your voice, gestures and expressions, using sensors such as cameras and microphones.

CAUGHT IN THE NET

Can you imagine a world without email, websites or instant messaging? Just 15 years ago, email was only used by the army and scientists, and the World Wide Web hadn't even been invented. Today, 500 million people all over the world use the Internet for entertainment, communication and information.

Cold connection

Internet connections can be installed into almost any household product. You can already buy an Internet Refrigerator, which has a computer on its door, a digital calendar to track your schedule and a camcorder for leaving video messages. You can use the refrigerator to email, surf the Web, download MP3 music, play DVDs and watch TV. It also tracks food supplies and will warn you when you're running low on anything.

The purple lines on this globe show Internet connections in the United States – the country with the most Internet users. In 2004, over 200 million people in the US had Internet connections at home.

Speed freak

Waiting and waiting for audio and video files to download could be a thing of the past now that researchers have come up with Fast TCP. This is an Internet connection that is 153,000 times faster than a modem. With Fast TCP, an entire movie can be downloaded in under five seconds.

Space net

Soon, the Internet could link to outer space. Information from space probes and astronauts could be sent to Earth using the same type of Internet communication that you use to send instant messages to your friends. This would make communication between space and Earth over 20,000 times faster than it is today. People would also be able to see clearer images of planets and even go on virtual missions to outer space from the comfort of their living rooms.

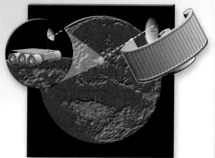

Information from machines exploring Mars could be sent to satellites orbiting the planet. The satellites would have an Internet link to Earth.

Antennas on Earth would receive the information from the satellites, 20,000 times faster than they do with existing technology.

Cyber criminals

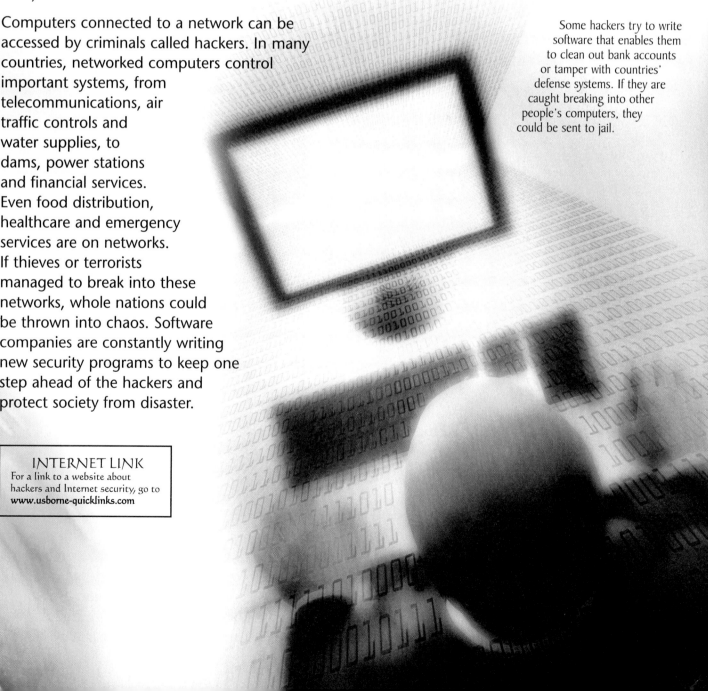

Computers connected to a network can be accessed by criminals called hackers. In many countries, networked computers control important systems, from telecommunications, air traffic controls and water supplies, to dams, power stations and financial services. Even food distribution, healthcare and emergency services are on networks. If thieves or terrorists managed to break into these networks, whole nations could be thrown into chaos. Software companies are constantly writing new security programs to keep one step ahead of the hackers and protect society from disaster.

Some hackers try to write software that enables them to clean out bank accounts or tamper with countries' defense systems. If they are caught breaking into other people's computers, they could be sent to jail.

INTERNET LINK
For a link to a website about hackers and Internet security, go to
www.usborne-quicklinks.com

THINKING COMPUTERS

Computers can carry out lots of instructions very quickly, but the quickest and most complicated instruction-processing system in the world is the human brain. Researchers are trying to create computers that "think" in a similar way to humans.

Robocup

Every July, soccer teams from all over the world compete in a huge tournament. This may sound like the World Cup, but there is one important difference – the players are all robots, programmed to think like soccer players. They must decide for themselves where to kick the ball and how to work as a team.

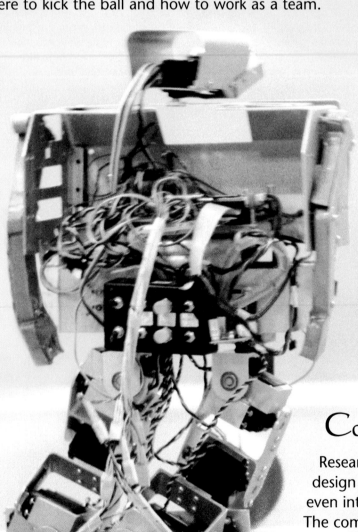

The organizers of the robot soccer tournament hope that, by 2050, a team of robots like these will have beaten the world's best human team.

Computer scientist

Researchers have programmed a computer to design laboratory experiments, carry them out, and even interpret the data, all without any human help. The computer controls a robot arm that can do the physical work, like holding test tubes and pouring liquids. Its inventors are hoping that, in the future, the computer will make new scientific discoveries.

Checkmate

In 2003, the world's most advanced chess computer program, X3D Fritz, took on the world's best chess player, Garry Kasparov, for the title of Man-Machine World Champion. The games were played in X3D virtual reality, with the board appearing to float in the air in front of Kasparov. To move the pieces, Kasparov simply told the computer what moves he wanted to make. Four games were played in all. The result? A tie. Kasparov and Fritz won two games each and had to share the title.

Electronic emotion

Jeremiah is a computer program that suffers from mood swings. This interactive virtual head can be downloaded onto a PC, where he will respond to what is happening around him. If nothing is happening, he looks sad, but waving at him will soon bring a smile to his face. Sudden movements surprise him, but when he sees an object that isn't moving, he'll assume it's ignoring him and become angry. He will happily follow a moving object with his eyes, but doing this for too long will make him bored.

This picture shows just some of the moods Jeremiah – an interactive virtual head – can express.

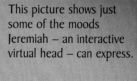

INTERNET LINK
For a link to a website where you can watch Jeremiah, the virtual head, go to www.usborne-quicklinks.com

Watching the skies

A team of astronomers has developed a computer program that keeps a constant watch on the sky. Using a network of telescopes linked over the Internet, the program can sift through sky observations, comparing them to previous images of the same region. It can decide whether it has spotted something interesting enough for further study and, if it has, will make more observations. In the future, the program will be able to take live action pictures of any interesting events it has seen and send them to astronomers' mobile phones.

When an asteroid moves across the sky, a telescope could spot it, turn on its video camera...

...and send a live-action picture of the asteroid to an astronomer's mobile phone.

83

RISE OF THE ROBOTS

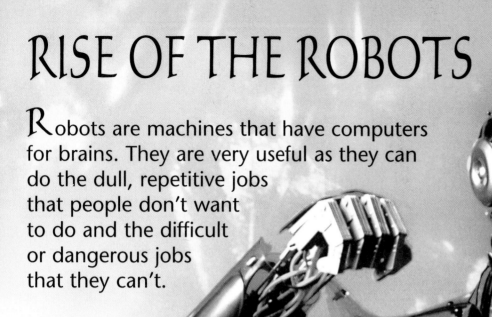

Robots are machines that have computers for brains. They are very useful as they can do the dull, repetitive jobs that people don't want to do and the difficult or dangerous jobs that they can't.

Helpful humanoids

Some robots are built to look and act like very helpful humans. Chatty humanoid robots can give out information about events in museums and theme parks. Some can also give directions, make small talk about the weather and fashion, and even ask for a cup of tea. To make them seem even more human, they can be programmed to show moods such as friendliness, fright, curiosity, irritation and boredom.

This humanoid robot can act as a tour guide and interactive information kiosk.

Robot butler

Scientists are developing a robot that will act as a personal assistant. The robot, called Cardea, can already recognize a door, roll up to it and open it with its one arm. Cardea will eventually have three arms, each one with a different attachment. One could carry objects, such as groceries, and another could unscrew jars and bottles.

Cardea currently looks like this...

... but may eventually look like this.

Walking chair

In the future, wheelchairs could be replaced by robot walking chairs. The WL-16 robot has two feet and is strong enough to carry a person. It can walk forward, backward and sideways and even go up and down steps. At the moment, it is radio-controlled but its inventors hope to fit it with a joystick that can be controlled by the user.

 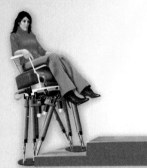

The WL-16 walks smoothly, even if its user moves about in the chair.

The robot can even carry its user up and down stairs.

Spy snake

Not all robots are designed to look and act like humans – some are based on animals. A snake robot has been developed that can act as a spy, with a video camera and broadcast system. The robot can be dropped from a helicopter onto a battlefield and will wiggle along the ground like a real snake until it reaches its destination. But, unlike a real snake, the robot will keep moving even if it gets damaged.

Wires run through the robot's body, supplying it with power and allowing it to slither along the ground like a snake.

Robot swarm

Tiny robots, the size of insects, could be swarming over the fields and factories of the future. They could be used to carry out checks and repairs inside complex or delicate machinery, to search buildings for chemical and biological weapons, or to locate and disable land mines.

This robot is fitted with a temperature sensor. Future versions could have a chemical sensor, camera, microphone, and communication device. The sweetcorn it is sitting on gives you an idea of just how small it is.

INTERNET LINK
For a link to a website where you can build your own virtual robot, go to www.usborne-quicklinks.com

SMALL WONDERS

Can you imagine something that is only one millionth of a millimeter long? Using the most powerful microscopes, scientists are able not only to see particles that are this tiny but also to use them to make materials and machines. Using particles in this way is called nanotechnology.

Smart dust

Scientists are developing microscopic devices, the size of a grain of sand, to act as miniature detectives. Called smart dust, the machines could be used to find impurities in drinking water, poisonous gases in the air and even cancerous cells in the human body. Smart dust already exists in the form of tiny sensors that are just millimeters long. They can monitor motion, temperature, and levels of light and radiation.

The pollution-detectors of the future may look like this – tiny machines so small that they would be able to fit through the eye of a needle.

Nanowhiskers

Nanotechnology can be put to use anywhere, even on your clothes. Tiny carbon hairs called nanowhiskers have been invented to help messy eaters stay stain-free. Natural fabrics, like cotton, can be covered with the hairs. They trap air in between them, similar to the hairs on your skin. When a liquid, such as ketchup, coffee or tea, falls onto the fabric, the trapped air props it up. The liquid forms into beads and rolls safely off the fabric.

Thanks to nanowhiskers, this spilled orange juice won't soak in to leave a stain. It forms into beads and rolls off the fabric.

Foggy future

Scientists could fill our future with fog – a fog made up of microscopic, twelve-armed machines. They could release the machines into the air and program them to join together in a variety of ways. Depending on how they join together, the machines could form almost any common objects, such as clothes, telephones, computers, cars and even houses.

Microscopic machines like these could be programmed to link arms to form materials of any shape or form.

This computer image shows how a nanobot might be used to inject medicines into an infected body cell.

Mini-motors

The world's smallest electrical device is a motor so tiny that 100 million of them could fit onto the end of a pin. In the future, the motor might be used to power tiny robots that could travel through your bloodstream to repair damaged cells or destroy tumors.

INTERNET LINK
For a link to a website where you can watch
a video-introduction to nanotechnology, go to
www.usborne-quicklinks.com

IN THE GENES

What all living things look like and how they function is determined largely by their genes. These are like instruction manuals inside each human, animal and plant. Genes are sections of DNA – a chemical code that stores whole libraries of information.

DNA detectives

Your DNA is unique. This means that, unless you have an identical twin, no other living thing has exactly the same chemical code as you. The police can use this fact to help them catch criminals. They search crime scenes for evidence such as hair, blood or saliva, which can be analyzed to find its DNA. If this matches DNA taken from a suspect, the police have strong evidence that the suspect was at the crime scene.

Although they look like weird, alien trees, these are hairs on a human head (the colors are added by computer). The root of each hair holds a genetic code specific to its owner.

Cracking the code

In 2000, a group of scientists announced that they had identified all the parts of the code for human life that is stored in human DNA. The code contains information about how a person is made and how he or she will grow and develop. Identifying all its parts was no easy task – it is around three billion letters long, with each letter representing one of four chemicals. Using the code, scientists hope to find out lots more about how the body works and what makes it go wrong. They have already discovered which genes contribute to asthma, diabetes and even migraines.

DNA has a long, thin shape like a twisted ladder. This computer model shows just a tiny section of DNA.

This pattern is a computer image of the code for a small sample of DNA. Each fragment of DNA is shown as a band of color.

Pass it on

When living things reproduce, their genes are passed on to their offspring. To influence what the next generation will look like, farmers and scientists can select the types of plant or animal they want to reproduce. For example, farmers might pick only the biggest animals to breed with each other, so that their young are more likely to be big too. This is called selective breeding.

You won't find hairless rats like this one in the wild – they are the result of selective breeding. Scientists use hairless rats to test medicines and cosmetics.

Cut and paste

Technology is now so advanced that scientists can "cut" a gene out of one plant or animal and "paste" it into another, to change the way this organism looks or behaves. This is called genetic engineering, or genetic modification, and has already brought lots of advances in farming and medicine. For example, tomato plants have been modified to be poisonous to the type of beetle that would normally eat them.

GM future?

Genetic engineers are working on many life-saving projects, such as modifying pig organs so they can be given to people who need organ transplants. But some people think that there should be laws restricting what scientists can do. This is because no one knows for certain what long-term effect genetically engineered products will have on people's health or on the environment.

INTERNET LINK
For a link to a website where you can explore a virtual genetically engineered world, go to
www.usborne-quicklinks.com

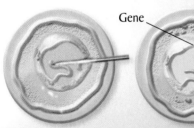

Gene

Genes are found inside cells – the tiny units that make up all living things. A gene can be taken out of a cell (shown here in yellow)...

... and placed inside a cell (shown here in blue) belonging to another living thing. The gene will affect the way the cell works in the future.

CLEVER CELLS

All living things, also called organisms, are made up of cells. Some simple organisms have just one cell, while complex organisms, like humans, have millions. Most cells contain DNA, which has all the information the cell needs to do its job. There is a whole branch of science dedicated to finding new ways to use cells in reproduction and to cure diseases.

Cloning around

Cloning is copying a living organism's DNA to create a new organism. In 1996, the first mammal clone – Dolly the sheep – was born. To make a lamb, you normally need a sperm cell from a male sheep and an egg cell from a female sheep. But scientists made Dolly in a laboratory by copying her mother's DNA. There was a problem, though. Because Dolly was born with exactly the same DNA as her six-year-old mother, her cells showed signs of early aging. Sheep usually live for 11 or 12 years, but Dolly died at the age of six, from lung disease, which is more common in older sheep.

Udder cell

Egg cell

Egg cell emptied of DNA

The nucleus, which holds DNA, is taken from a cell in the mother's udder and put into an emptied egg cell from another sheep. The egg is put into a third sheep. The lamb is a clone of the mother.

DNA is being taken out of an animal cell through a fine needle. Only DNA that is undamaged can be used to make new animals.

Why clone?

Cloning is useful in medical research, where scientists need to try out different experiments on organisms that have exactly the same genetic make-up. In the future, cloning might even be used to bring extinct animals back to life. We might not be walking around with dinosaurs right away though, as we would need to find a dinosaur's complete, undamaged DNA.

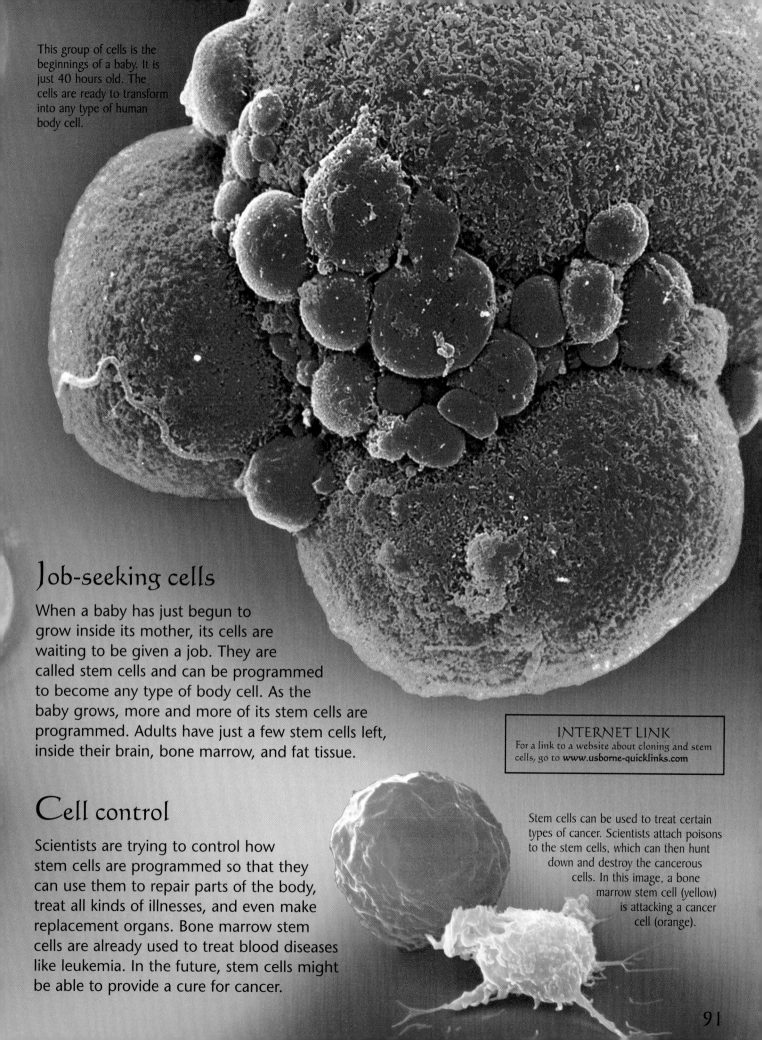

This group of cells is the beginnings of a baby. It is just 40 hours old. The cells are ready to transform into any type of human body cell.

Job-seeking cells

When a baby has just begun to grow inside its mother, its cells are waiting to be given a job. They are called stem cells and can be programmed to become any type of body cell. As the baby grows, more and more of its stem cells are programmed. Adults have just a few stem cells left, inside their brain, bone marrow, and fat tissue.

INTERNET LINK
For a link to a website about cloning and stem cells, go to www.usborne-quicklinks.com

Cell control

Scientists are trying to control how stem cells are programmed so that they can use them to repair parts of the body, treat all kinds of illnesses, and even make replacement organs. Bone marrow stem cells are already used to treat blood diseases like leukemia. In the future, stem cells might be able to provide a cure for cancer.

Stem cells can be used to treat certain types of cancer. Scientists attach poisons to the stem cells, which can then hunt down and destroy the cancerous cells. In this image, a bone marrow stem cell (yellow) is attacking a cancer cell (orange).

BODY MECHANICS

Over the past ten years, there have been huge advances in technology and in the knowledge of how the human body works. This is helping scientists to find new ways to combine human intelligence with the power of machines.

Robot bodies

Cyborgs are humans that have machine parts built into their bodies. This may sound like science fiction, but machines such as pacemakers, which keep the heart beating regularly, and artificial limbs are currently being fitted into humans to repair their bodies. The machines are controlled by electrical signals, also called impulses, that the body uses to send messages to and from the brain. In the future, people might be able to have computers fitted into their bodies to make their senses more powerful. They could even have very tiny computers injected into their bodies to repair damaged cells.

Electronic eel

Scientists have developed a robot that is controlled by the brain of an eel. The brain is kept alive in salty water and is attached to the robot by wires. It sends electrical signals to control the direction the robot moves. This research could help in the development of robotic body parts for stroke victims and others who suffer nerve damage.

Part-man, part-machine: in the future, parts of people's bodies could perhaps be replaced by machines, like this.

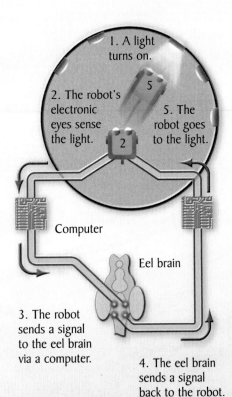

1. A light turns on.

2. The robot's electronic eyes sense the light.

5. The robot goes to the light.

Computer

Eel brain

3. The robot sends a signal to the eel brain via a computer.

4. The eel brain sends a signal back to the robot.

Mind over matter

Scientists have trained a monkey to control a robot arm using just the power of its mind. When the monkey thinks about moving an object, the electrical impulses from its brain are sent to a computer, which uses the impulses to move the robot arm. In the future, this method could be used to help paralyzed people move by sending their thought signals from a computerized implant in their brain to another one in their limb.

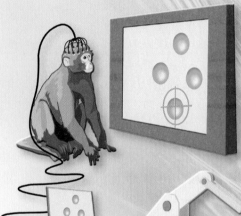

As the monkey thinks about moving an image of a ball on a screen, sensors attached to its head send electrical signals to a computer. The computer picks up the signals and uses them to make a robotic arm pick up the ball.

INTERNET LINK
For a link to a website about technology and the human body, go to www.usborne-quicklinks.com

This surfer is riding virtual ocean waves, created by a computer. His helmet is connected to the computer and controls what he sees and hears.

Virtual world

Virtual reality takes you into a world where everything you see, hear and – in the more advanced programs – feel is created by a computer. As computers become increasingly sophisticated, virtual worlds are becoming more realistic. The latest technology combines virtual reality with video cameras, so real people in different places can meet, talk to each other and even go shopping in a virtual environment.

93

INDEX

The numbers shown in **bold** type show where major subject areas are covered.

ACKNOWLEDGEMENTS

Cover designed by Neil Francis
Managing designer: Karen Tomlins
Digital imagery by Joanne Kirkby, Michael Hill,
Keith Furnival, Adam Constantine and Laura Hammonds

Website advisor: Lisa Watts
Editorial assistant: Valerie Findlay

Americanization by Carrie Armstrong

96